A LIFE WELL LIVED

Mrs. Dunning's Lesson Plan for Happiness

Published by Flourishing Media
Winston-Salem, NC
an imprint of Partners Media Publishing
New York, NY

Published with the generous support of
Dr. and Mrs. Malcolm Brown
Lynn and Barry Eisenberg
Mastroianni-Shaw Fund
Janie and J.D. Wilson
The Arts Council of Winston-Salem and Forsyth County

In association with
Fifth Letter
Excalibur Direct Marketing
Thomas L. Spry

Catalog-in-Publication Data is available
from the Library of Congress.

ISBN 9798993445205

Book design: Fifth Letter

To my students, who were my best teachers.
To my teachers, who made me a better student.
To my family and friends, who have been
the bedrock of my joyful experience.

A LIFE WELL LIVED

Mrs. Dunning's
Lesson Plan for Happiness

PRAISE FOR MRS. DUNNING

Passionate Heart & Dedication—*That* describes PHD: Phyllis Hemrick Dunning. A Purpose-driven Helper who Delivers opportunities and transforms lives through her unwavering commitment to arts and education. Her Purposeful Heartfelt Deeds extend beyond her former classroom, creating bridges between generations and cultures. At 92, she remains a Powerful, Hopeful Dynamo, serving on boards and championing causes. I have witnessed firsthand how this Perpetual Hope Distributor touches souls—one student/artist at a time.

—Jonathan Nicolas, Devoted Friend

Phyllis's deep appreciation of the arts is evident to anyone who knows her. She has inspired countless individuals to pursue their artistic dreams. Whether it's the opera, Broadway, the ballet, or a Shakespearean play, you will find Phyllis supporting the production from the front row. For those fortunate enough to know Phyllis Dunning, the world is a brighter and more intriguing place.

—Kait Lagalante, Great Granddaughter

Dressed to perfection, a smile that lights up those around her, and never a dull conversation: I am grateful to have Phyllis in my life, and the world is a better place because of her.

—Verla Hemrick, Niece by Marriage

When I first spent time with Mrs. Dunning, she told me wonderful stories of her life as a younger person who had travelled the world. I was fascinated by how much she could remember and the passion with which she recalled events that were meaningful to her. Over time, I have learned a great deal about Phyllis' life and how she lives it. Most notably, she lives her life to the fullest. Since meeting her, I have had the heartwarming experience of witnessing (firsthand) Phyllis' dedication to young artists. I am so grateful to have such a wonderful person invite me into her life and embrace my family.

—Veda Storey, Friend

When we moved to Winston-Salem, Phyllis took us under her wing, introducing us to all the various arts groups and helping us get involved. Her introductions led to a richer existence in our new home. We became so involved with organizations like UNCSA (University of North Carolina School of the Arts), Piedmont Opera, Winston-Salem Symphony, and Reynolda House that we really began to feel at home in Winston-Salem. Thanks to Phyllis' encouragement, we have found the perfect place to live out our days.

—Frank & Gary, Friends

Phyllis is an iconic English teacher, a keen intellect, a loving family person, a dedicated supporter and patron of the arts, an inspiring mentor, an outstanding community member, a loyal alumna of Salem College, and a caring friend. When you walk away from an encounter with Phyllis, you are uplifted. She is that rare individual who lives an authentic, positive, and loving existence, and she shares that energy with whomever she meets—she has the ability to make you a better person. Phyllis Dunning is a blessing. I believe we should all be calling her: The Arts Angel.

—Libby Trull, Friend

I love Phyllis Dunning. Not only did Phyllis take me to Salem College, the School of the Arts, the Piedmont Opera, and the Winston-Salem Symphony as her guest, but she also introduced me to everybody involved. She shared her network of friends, which reaches far and wide! Phyllis is a guiding light for so many people. And rather than dwelling on the impact she's had on others, she focuses on the impact they have had on her. Phyllis is a treasure.

—Sandy Romanac Broadway, Friend and Neighbor

I have over 60 years of memories of Aunt Phyllis. All of Phyllis's nieces and nephews had the privilege of going on one of her European tours during high school. Time spent with Aunt Phyllis is often a time of firsts. Indeed, whenever I want to know about the hottest up-and-coming show, I reach out to Aunt Phyllis. While she didn't birth children of her own, Aunt Phyllis impacted the lives of hundreds, if not thousands, of children through her high school teaching days and beyond.

—Don Hemrick Jr., Nephew

My grandmother, Phyllis Dunning, has always been my cultural "guru." At seventeen, as an early graduation gift for me, Phyllis sponsored (and chaperoned) an epic trip to Europe. This opened my mind and my world as she taught me that travel can facilitate cultural experiences which fill one's soul through art, music, history, and exploration. This valuable lesson was a transformative gift (given to me at a young age), and it has been fostered throughout my life. She continues to inspire and amaze, and I feel grateful and blessed that we are family.

—Dana Troemel, Granddaughter

Phyllis embodies the importance of the arts in the eyes of everyone who knows her. She shares her wealth of knowledge and her belief that the arts offer transformational opportunities for every young person. Whether attending a fundraising event or just offering wise counsel over lunch or morning coffee, Phyllis enhances and expands the sustainability of vital work like Authoring Action. Phyllis knows how important it is to bolster the development of struggling teens who are learning how to express themselves with pen and paper, or the adults whose voices and stories bring important insights for the wholeness of our community.

—Lynn Rhoades, Co-Founder/Executive Director
Authoring Action, authoringaction.org

To know Phyllis Dunning is to know the heart and soul of Winston-Salem. Her influence extends far beyond individual relationships, touching neighborhoods, organizations, and the community as a whole.

As she has for so many others, Phyllis introduced me to the arts in unforgettable ways: taking me to my first opera, my first Symphony performance, and even my first visit to The Metropolitan Museum of Art in New York City. Her example has inspired me to give generously of my time and talents and to remain engaged in the arts. Her personal motto, "Life is about choices and attitudes," reminds me that, regardless of circumstances, we can shape our own paths by the way we choose to think and act.

—Katie Hall Nicolas, Devoted Friend

CONTENTS

FOREWORD

A tall, tan thermos stands atop a desk pad calendar displaying the month of May. Left of the thermos (which covers most of the month's days, leaving only a few dates—all punctuated with reminders—visible), sits a desk-podium, its slanted wood top covered with lesson notes, brochures for the opera and symphony, and the editorial page of the *Winston-Salem Journal*.

Tucked almost out of sight, within the lectern's cubby, is the *New York Times* Daily Crossword inked audaciously with bold capital answers. In front of the thermos and to the right of the lectern stands a tabletop bookshelf, filled with volumes of Chaucer, Spenser, Shakespeare, Blake, Milton, Swift, and Dickens.

This is the nerve center of our beloved and awe-inspiring English teacher, Mrs. Dunning (or "Mrs. D," as affectionately called by a fortunate few).

Seconds before the end of the previous busy period, Mrs. D swoops-in to take her place at the lectern. She is a statuesque woman, and though she is not wealthy, she is dressed to the nines in a striking wool crepe gold suit, accompanied by an Hermès scarf featuring floating yellow keys that dance across her shoulders. She exudes an air of European royalty, with a cresting wave of sweeping auburn hair blown back, revealing an impressive forehead that just screams "genius." And yet, when she smiles (which is often), she evokes a warm, protective feeling—the kind of feeling you might have for the protagonist of an Elizabeth Spencer novel.

This morning, a grin (more mischievous than that belonging to the Cheshire Cat) spreads across her face from ear to ear. It disappears as she downs one last sip of coffee from her lipstick-covered cup. Lifting her gold-rimmed glasses from the folds of her cream-colored silk blouse to the bridge of her nose, she glances at her watch and so begins our lesson...

I have just described the person who has penned the beautiful words of sage wisdom you will find in this book; she is a person whom I would follow to the ends of the earth. To convey the profound influence she has had on thousands of students would require a much larger tome, as weighty and as ambitious in size and scope as *War and Peace*. She is one of those rare combinations of intelligence, warmth, and *joie de vivre*. And trust me: if Phyllis Dunning is dishing out advice, it's worth listening to.

Yet, this book is so much more than advice. Phyllis has always led and continues to lead by example. Her anecdotes are as honest as they are enlightening. It is indeed a timely and priceless gift that she has chosen to share with us now. One would be wise to sit up and take notes.

In a world that moves faster with each passing day, it's easy to feel like you're falling behind—trapped by your own habits, fears, or the pressure to keep up. We often search for guidance outside of ourselves, hoping someone will hand us a roadmap amid the confusion.

What you're holding now is more than a book; it's Mrs. Dunning's book. The consummate teacher, who somehow seems all-knowing in her wisdom, with a calm, nurturing, guiding hand. It's a mirror, a compass, and a conversation with someone who understands that the journey to personal growth is both deeply individual and profoundly universal.

This book doesn't claim to have all the answers—and that's precisely what makes it powerful. Instead, through its tapestry of stories, sprinklings of humor, and loving touch, it offers tools, perspectives, and gentle challenges to help you ask better questions. It's written not to fix you, but to remind you that you were never broken to begin with.

Whether you are navigating a significant life transition, striving to adopt better habits, or simply seeking to feel more like yourself again, this book is a companion for the path ahead. It invites you to pause, reflect, and reconnect—with your values, your vision, and your voice.

Read it with curiosity. Return to it with courage. And most of all, allow it to spark the change that you already carry within.

— Michael Wilson, Broadway Director,
Grateful Student & Fan of Mrs. Dunning,
and Inquisitive, Reflective Student of Life

INTRODUCTION

It was the best of times, it was the worst of times, it was the age of wisdom, it was the age of foolishness, it was the epoch of belief, it was the epoch of incredulity, it was the season of Light, it was the season of Darkness, it was the spring of hope, it was the winter of despair.

—Charles Dickens, *A Tale of Two Cities*

June 18, 1933: the day I entered this wonderful world. The global landscape looked different upon my arrival than it does today. As Dickens aptly wrote, "It was the best of times, it was the worst of times." That year, 1933, was one of the worst years of the Great Depression. Dust bowls blanketed the Midwest; earthquakes hit both Japan and California; Adolf Hitler was named Chancellor of Germany; the first Nazi concentration camp, Dachau, was completed.

Yet, despite so much upheaval in the world, there was also triumph: Air France was formed; the Toyota company was started in Japan; the Twenty-First Amendment repealed prohibition; Mahatma Gandhi began a twenty-one-day fast in protest for Indian independence.

Newsweek magazine was first published in the United States; the first singing telegram was introduced in New York City; the Irish parliament abolished the Oath of Allegiance to the British Crown; Edwin Howard Armstrong invented FM radio; Alan Blumlein invented stereo records; and Franklin D. Roosevelt opened the White House swimming pool.

Among the hit songs of the day were "Night and Day" by Eddy Duchin, "Stormy Weather" by Ethel Waters, and "You're Getting to Be a Habit with Me" by Bing Crosby with Guy Lombardo's Royal Canadians. Several classic movies were released, including *Alice in Wonderland, Little Women,* and *King Kong.* On the sports front, England's Wally Hammond scored a record 336 runs in a cricket match against

New Zealand; the first Major League Baseball all-star game was played in Chicago; and the Bears beat the Giants in the National Football League's first scheduled championship game at Chicago's Wrigley Field.

I joined the world along with many notable 1933 babies: Sir Michael Caine, Quincy Jones, Joan Rivers, Gene Wilder, James Brown, Yoko Ono, Nina Simone, Elizabeth Montgomery, and Joan Collins, as well as several emperors, presidents, Nobel Prize winners, and poets.

Much happened in 1933; much happens every year. Even more happens in a decade or a quarter of a century—and an extraordinary amount happens in an entire century. As I edge closer to becoming a centenarian and reflect on the many changes the world has seen in my lifetime, I am also struck by what has remained steadfast. Humanity is resilient. When life is good, we thrive; when it is not, we sometimes crumble under pressure. However, we often rise higher than we thought possible.

Yes, a lot has changed since 1933, yet nothing has changed. Even with the advent of AI, the basic constructs that make humanity *human* still exist: creativity, passion, courage, empathy, integrity, curiosity, and so much more.

Over my ninety-plus years, I have learned many lessons. As I survey our society, one of my observations is that people have become increasingly stressed. With technological advances moving at lightning speed and global information constantly bombarding our psyches, there is a perceived inability to "unplug" and retreat to a calm personal center. Today's work culture often perpetuates this pressure to be available no matter where you are. Our collective modern tech addiction has fueled the flame of feeling overwhelmed and out of control. Many of the stressors in modern life are beyond our control: natural disasters, global hunger (though we can always help), the ever-fragile international political landscape, war, and tyranny. The list is lengthy. These stressors have been in the world since my early life and long before that. The difference today is that we stream them in real time. Constant information grabs our minds and engages us in the day's conflict.

Although social media is a marvelous way to keep up with friends, family, and even world events (I am a big fan of it for this reason), this same "wonderful innovation" is also fraught with conflict, cyber cruelty, and more advertisements than one can digest. Anonymity allows people to post things that they would never say in person. Disinformation and misinformation have been problems since the beginning of these platforms. Social media provides a mechanism by which misinformation can travel at breakneck speed. A 2018 study published in *Science* by MIT researchers Sorough Vosoughi, Deb Roy, and Sinan Aral found that misinformation can spread up to ten times faster than factual reporting, and the problem is increasing. Unfortunately, exciting stories always overshadow facts. It is so prevalent that there is a term for it: "viral spread."

Artificial intelligence has sparked a global conversation. Conversation and dialogue are positive in any form, but the constant bombardment of fearful messaging is not. This type of conversation regarding AI (or any other major societal issue) fuels anxiety about job security and where this unprecedented technology will take us. I am not suggesting hiding our heads in the sand like an ostrich. Knowledge of world events is imperative, but a constant diet of fear-evoking messaging is unhealthy.

So, how do we navigate this "brave new world" and balance our lives in this climate?

Each day, when we wake up, we must do so thoughtfully. The first five minutes of our waking state are critical. It's a new day, and we have a clean slate. We make choices that either positively set our intention or leave us to the mercy of chance, setting us up to be reactive instead of proactive. We can see the best of the world or the worst of it. There is plenty to see through either lens. I choose to see the best. I start every day with gratitude. Anyone can do this and I highly recommend it.

There will always be a struggle. There will always be war or the threat of war, climate change, a pandemic, or any of the thousands of other issues that make this world a daunting place. So, how do we combat these imminent and ever-present threats to our well-being?

Humanity's inherent principles, ideals, and beliefs help men, women, and children thrive in this wonderful, conflicted world we call home.

Today, we seek comfort and solace in community, the arts, and education. These three things are vital to the fabric and heartbeat of our culture. They nurture us, help us grow, and lift us when needed. They provide peace, understanding, and hope. This powerful trinity is available to everyone.

The trajectory of *my* journey has also been influenced by my biggest role models: my parents. A brief description of their impact on my life might illuminate how I have absorbed the values and lessons they shared with me—values and lessons which I continue to uphold to this day, and which I will share with you in the hope that they will be helpful and enlightening.

As you forge your path, I hope some of the truths I've learned and the insights I've acquired will help guide you. Take a breath and pause to absorb the magnificent view of your journey.

LESSON 1

MY PARENTS

My heroes are and were my parents. I can't see having anyone else as my heroes.

—Michael Jordan

I had terrific parents. They gave my siblings and me a strong foundation for our lives, and I am profoundly thankful for them. I was the eldest of five children (and in my opinion, the most spoiled!). Then came Don two and a half years later. Bonnie was born eight years after that, followed by Rick and Bob. I was a teenager by the time Rick and Bob came along. We were a close-knit family and remained so throughout our lives.

Early childhood development is critical and shapes so much of who we become as adults. One of my happiest childhood memories is of my whole family singing in the car. Wherever we went, we sang!

My mother was a very positive person and a great confidence builder. Mother convinced us: "You can do everything. You can do anything." With that kind of encouragement, our world was full of infinite possibilities and potential.

When you're young, you're naive enough to accept the words of your parents without question, so it never dawned on me that I couldn't do whatever I set my mind to. *And you can too.* If you have no voice inside of you contradicting your choices, the world is your oyster. Mother gave me that gift; I have carried it my whole life.

My dad was a wonderful, thoughtful person and cared deeply for all of us, though he was not quite as positive as Mother. But his doubts were never about his family. I remember when Mr. Gordon Hanes, the owner of the hosiery factory where my Dad worked, offered my father a promotion. There was a specific job that he wanted Dad to do. Dad came home and told Mother about it.

I overheard them talking, and Dad said, "You know, I just really don't know that I'm the person for that job."

I remember Mother replying, "What three people at the plant could do that better than you?"

Dad responded, "Well, I don't know . . ."

"What *two* people can do it?"

Dad shook his head, unable to think of viable candidates.

"Anybody?" Mother asked, "Is there *anybody* who would be better at that job than you?"

Dad laughed and said, "Well, I guess when you put it that way . . ."

Mother ended the discussion, "Gordon Hanes knows what he's doing. He knows you're the best person for that job."

Mother knew. Mother always knew.

She had discovered two great tenets of successful people: positivity and confidence. The belief in one's ability is a powerful force. It puts you in the driver's seat, allowing you to be proactive and consciously shape your life's path. I will always admire my mother. She was tenacious and full of light.

The compliment I most treasure when I receive it is, "You remind me of your mother."

Her love and guidance remind me of a William Henry Channing poem, *My Symphony*:

> To live content with small means;
> To seek elegance rather than luxury, and refinement rather than fashion;
> To be worthy, not merely respectable, and wealthy, not rich;
> To listen to stars and birds, babes and sages with open heart;
> To study hard;
> To think quietly, act frankly, talk gently, await occasions, hurry never;
> In a word, to let the spiritual, unbidden, and unconscious, grow up through the common—this is my symphony.

These are words to live by, and these words represent Mother's beliefs through and through. My mother only ever had one shortcoming that I discovered. When I went off to college I called her in a panic.

"Mother," I said frantically, "you taught me a lot of valuable things, but you never taught me how to do my hair! It is a mess! I don't know what to do with it!"

I would always shampoo my own hair, but then Mother would curl it and roll it. Then, when it was dry, she would comb and style it. Mother loved to dress up children! Despite this oversight in my education, she talked me through my hair crisis and the world kept turning.

I admired my father for different reasons. Dad was more tentative. Reflecting on his family and the way he grew up, I can see why he might have been less confident. As a youth, Dad had a lot of potential, and a doctor in the community wanted to send him to Wake Forest University. But Dad was the eldest boy and shouldered a lot of responsibility that kept him from pursuing a medical education. He had three sisters, two older and one younger, and three brothers. Two big fires broke out on their large farm when the children were still young. One burned their house, and the other burned both their house and their barn. Even though the doctor I mentioned wanted to send Dad to Wake Forest, Dad felt it was his duty to help his family recover from the great losses caused by the two fires. It was a noble and great sacrifice for him to turn down the opportunity for an education, but there was so much to rebuild on the farm that he simply could not abandon what he saw as his duty. So, when Dad finished high school, he got a job with Hanes Hosiery.

My dad's lack of confidence stemmed partly from his awareness that he did not have a post-secondary education. However, he rolled up his sleeves and made the best of his chosen path. He was a hard worker and learned how to do his job to the best of his ability. His strong work ethic served him well, and by the end of the summer, he'd already received a raise at the factory.

The Hanes' were a prominent family in the area: hardworking, extremely successful, and well-respected. Mr. Jim Hanes, the company's founder, liked my father a lot. Dad was an excellent quail and duck hunter, and over the years, when Mr. Hanes got a new hunting dog, he would bring it to my dad, saying, "Okay, Paul, I want you to train my dog."

That was an honor for my father which he had earned because of his evident good character—my dad knew who he was and who he was choosing to be. Despite his limited education, my father succeeded in many ways. As Mark Twain reminded us, education is only sometimes gleaned in a classroom.

As a teenager, Mr. Hanes's son, Gordon Hanes, attended prep school at Woodberry Forest School in Virginia. When he was fifteen years old and home for the summer, Gordon came to the plant with his father, who said to my dad, "Mr. Paul, if I put this young whippersnapper with you for the summer, do you think you could teach him anything?"

Dad said, "I'd love to do that."

So, my father became a teacher and a mentor. Though Dad first became close to Gordon when he was a teenager, they remained friends for all of Gordon's life. They would go hunting and fishing and spend quality time together outside of work.

Besides his skill at work, my dad was also very athletic. He was an excellent baseball player. As an adult, he played on the Hanes Hosiery team in the textile league. They would play teams from North Carolina, South Carolina, and Virginia, and Dad excelled on the field. I've seen photographs from when he and my mother were dating. He was handsome and athletic looking then.

When my brothers were growing up, my dad was the Little League coach for baseball and basketball, and he was devoted (once again) to his duties. He was the parent who organized the boys into teams; he was their chauffeur and coach; he did everything with them. He nurtured my brothers, encouraging their talents and their growth.

Not content to enjoy baseball alone, my father also became an excellent golfer. When his friends taught him, they would say, "He can hit a golf ball like he is hitting a baseball. He just knocked the hell out of that ball!"

As a result of my dad's guidance and love of athletics, my brothers grew up on Little League baseball and basketball teams, playing golf, and taking tennis lessons.

I, on the other hand, was an athletic failure. We had a basketball hoop in the backyard, and Dad would say, "It's time for everyone to get outside and exercise."

He always said he could round everybody up except for me. Everyone knew that when the time came to engage in sports, Phyllis would grab a book and hide.

Although I was not a natural athlete, Dad was very nurturing and appreciated my love of reading and literature. He wasn't an avid book reader himself. He read books, but he was busy with so many other things. He read newspapers, magazines, *Time, Life, Newsweek, The Saturday Evening Post,* and *Sports Illustrated*. He may not have had a formal education, but he did his best to educate himself.

He'd tell me, "Now, Phi-Phi, I like that you like to read"—and Dad liked to read, too, he'd say—"But you need more outside and exercise. That's important, too."

Later, I realized he was right. I was not physically coordinated when I tried to play golf, tennis, or ski, and I did not naturally excel at any of those. My brothers, as I've mentioned, were natural athletes.

The one athletic endeavor I really enjoyed was riding our pony, Ginger. I rode Ginger in the yard or the neighborhood, sometimes to a friend's house. We had two ponies, Ginger and her foal, Patchie. Ginger was a five-gait pony. My brother, Don, used to show her in competitions. She was amazing! We all rode. Mother and Dad built a house just outside the Winston-Salem city limits near where Wake Forest University now stands (ponies were not allowed within the city limits).

When Winston-Salem annexed that area and rezoned it, Dad said, "Children need to grow up with ponies!" and he and Mother purchased land on Shattalon Drive, where they built a new house on eight acres of land. The original parcel of land was larger, but they sold a great deal of it to finance our new home.

Dad had his own five-gaited horse that he really enjoyed. Though he was not a polo player, he kept his horse at the polo stables on Polo Road. The stables are now long gone, replaced by a school.

Sometimes, Dad would leave the plant, go straight to the polo stables and ride the horse to our house. If we were playing in the yard and saw him coming, we'd run to the porch for safety! His horse was very feisty! She was a lot of horse to handle, but Daddy (as I have said) had grown up on a farm and he was accustomed to horses. We children stuck to riding ponies.

Dad had a promising career. Hanes was an excellent company, and my dad did well at his job, but he was always a salaried employee. With a wife and five children, money didn't go far; however, Mother and Dad were a strong team. Dad earned the money and (thank heavens!) Mother managed it. Dad was a word person, and Mother was a numbers person. She could stretch a dollar further than most people could stretch twenty. As a result, we led a comfortable life.

When Dad retired, she told all of us, Dad included, "Your father is accustomed to being in charge, and now, I'm the only person he has that he can supervise. And, in my opinion, this is not working well!"

She decided to get a job, and became an excellent hostess in various buildings in Old Salem. She worked there for fifteen years, loving every minute of it. She would greet visitors to the site and share the history of the place with them. She'd come home and regale us with stories of the most wonderful people she'd met that day—a gentleman from Connecticut, elementary children from Kernersville, the nicest couple from Denmark. She was in her glory!

Dad used to joke that Old Salem didn't pay her enough to cover the gas it cost to go down there, but he knew she was happy, and that was what was important.

When Mother and Dad celebrated their golden wedding anniversary, fifty beautiful years, we had a big celebration at our home, with friends and loved ones. We gave a great deal of thought as to what to get them to celebrate such a monumental occasion. We wanted something very meaningful and ultimately decided to commission a framed painting of our beautiful homestead where they had nurtured and raised us with patience and love. Along with that, we each wrote them letters, some of the grandchildren made drawings, and we bound them into a book for our parents to keep. We had a wonderful time creating it and my parents loved it more than they would have loved a trip around the world.

As an introduction to their gift we wrote:

> This is the stuff of which dreams are made. You have been our major role models, living examples of faith, hope and love. Without playing favorites, you somehow make each of us feel a very favored one. We honor and thank you on this fiftieth anniversary of your life together with these expressions of just some of our love and gratitude. How blessed we all are to have you!

We used to tell Mother and Dad, "You've loved us, educated us, housed us, fed us, taught us to be responsible. As far as we're concerned, don't save any money for us. Go out with your last dime. Enjoy. You've done for us and taught us how to do for ourselves. Now, do for you, and don't worry about leaving anything." We all felt that way.

Dad lived to be ninety-four. Months before he passed, the doctor had told him, "You're more like seventy-something than you are ninety-something." He had no dementia. He remembered everything. At ninety-four, he was walking to a friend's place for dinner when he was tragically struck by a car and killed instantly. My siblings and I chose to believe our father died happily, anticipating a good meal and good conversation.

I learned a lot from my parents, but more than anything, I learned to take control of my mind. *The way you think dictates your life*—it truly does. It is the difference between success and failure. *If you think you can, you can. If you think you can't, you have already failed.*

If you are simply reactive to life, you are not truly on a rewarding path. Pick a lane and drive in it for a while. See where it leads you. You can always get off at the next exit and try another route if it doesn't feel right. Your path may be more complex than most people's. You can zig and then zag and have enriching experiences along the way, but only if you are awake enough to see them.

My dad picked his lane and drove in that lane to the best of his ability. Both of my parents did an excellent job raising us. Starting with a strong foundation makes a huge difference in one's life.

Perhaps you were not fortunate enough to grow up in a loving home with two nurturing parents to guide you. That may make your beginning wobbly, but with thoughtful reflection, you can learn from your past, whatever that may be. My father's literal foundation was struck down twice in two different fires, yet he persevered and thrived.

It is often said that "we can only play the hand that is dealt to us," but *we have the power of choice*. Play your cards with thoughtful deliberation as my father did, and like him, you can strengthen your foundation. And if you decide to have children, give your children the tools to make their foundations withstand the storms of life.

LESSON 2

ARTS AND EDUCATION

It is art that makes life, makes interest, makes importance... and I know of no substitute whatever for the force and beauty of its process.

—Henry James

The arts and education are of utmost importance, especially when geared toward young people, because young people are the future. They're a blank canvas filled with optimism and potential.

As a high school English teacher, I dedicated my career to nurturing students and expanding their minds. I realized that I had an opportunity and responsibility to positively impact their lives within the walls of my classroom so they could make a difference beyond the classroom. Through the years, thousands of students have graced the desks of my English class, and I made it my mission to introduce each of them to great works of literature.

Language is a powerful medium. It can clarify and deceive, probe and soothe the mind and spirit, express the vivid and the vague, evoke chuckles, tears, and shivers, and etch wrinkles on the brow and brain. To develop skill and understanding in the use of language is to claim a priceless inheritance.

Literature has an unparalleled ability to illuminate the depths of our human experience. Transcending time and culture, the written word fosters understanding and tolerance as readers step into the shoes of people from diverse backgrounds. It explores the complexities of the human condition and offers insights into our collective hopes and fears, joys and sorrows.

Literature is also a potent vehicle for change. It challenges social norms and provides a platform for marginalized voices. It can inspire, transporting readers to realms beyond their everyday lives. The power of literature lies in its ability to shape and enrich our understanding of the world, serving as a timeless testament to humanity's shared essence.

My passion for language and literature is rivaled only by my passion for teaching. Education is so much more than a pathway to a better-paying job. It is a conduit to a world of enrichment and fulfillment.

Einstein expressed it best when he declared the actual value of education to be "not the learning of many facts, but the training of the mind to think."

Education wields a transformative power extending far beyond the confines of the classroom. It catalyzes personal and societal advancement and forms the foundation for intellectual development. It equips individuals with knowledge, critical thinking skills, and vital tools to navigate the complexities of the modern world.

Beyond its many cognitive benefits, education champions a sense of empowerment. It enables students to make informed choices and contribute meaningfully to their communities. Education is a potent force for social mobility, breaking down barriers and providing opportunities to transcend socioeconomic limitations.

In its broadest sense, education is a beacon of enlightenment, promoting tolerance, understanding, and a shared sense of humanity. Education empowers people by allowing them to acquire information and by cultivating well-rounded, empathetic people poised to shape the future positively.

Along with education, I'm convinced that the arts civilize us. It's through art that we can be unified. Art is a necessary, vital part of society. In many ways, art is society's "canary in the coalmine." Artists breathe in the world and breathe out wisdom and insights into past, present, and future before anyone else has processed it. They are a warning signal. They're our barometer. They provide a roadmap that gives meaning to our lives. They are not a frill or an extra. They are as vital as the air we breathe.

The arts play a fundamental role in our society. A robust reflection of our collective humanity, they ignite cultural, intellectual, spiritual, and emotional enrichment. Beyond their aesthetic value, the arts support the development of creativity, empathy, and discernment. They foster a deep understanding of diverse perspectives, creating connections that transcend boundaries. The arts are the cornerstone of a vibrant and flourishing society. They provide a unique and essential vehicle for interpreting, expressing, and celebrating the complexities of the human experience. And art can guide and nurture us in difficult times.

Nine days after the tragic events of September 11, 2001, the members of the New York Philharmonic went back to work as essential workers. Fresh off a European tour and flying into an eerily silent New York, they answered the moral call to help respond to and relieve mass grief in search of a place to land and to heal. They had planned to open their season with a festive program, but in light of the horrific terror attacks that had paralyzed the world, the planned concerts were not possible. Maestro Kurt Masur planned the program for that most critical and monumental performance. He understood that the Philharmonic needed to hit the right note, conveying both memoriam and a much-needed message of hope. He searched for a vehicle to uplift and console. He chose the most potent piece he could find, a masterpiece Johannes Brahms had written over a century earlier to comfort the living after loss: *A German Requiem*. There was not a dry eye in Lincoln Center that evening of September 20, 2001, as the New York Philharmonic performed this masterpiece.

Art has great power. To paraphrase the French National Convention in the midst of the French Revolution (and popularized by Uncle Ben in *Spider-Man*): "With great power comes great responsibility."

The incredibly talented and spiritual musician Sting lost a friend in the Twin Towers that fateful day. Yet he answered the same call in his backyard in Tuscany on the evening of 9/11. Foregoing a concert previously planned for that night, he and his band carefully considered the "right" thing to do. After much discussion and soul-searching, they felt they needed to address all those who desperately needed music's cleansing power. The result was a hauntingly soulful and intimate performance for guests in a beautiful outdoor setting, later televised as a poignant gift to the world.

Many other musicians also answered the call at that time. Songs like Bruce Springsteen's "Into The Fire" and Jay-Z's "Empire State of Mind," featuring Alicia Keys, captured Americans' hearts and sensibilities.

Music finds, connects, transports, and transforms us in ways that words alone cannot. There is a reason it is called the universal language. Moreover, music and poetry have a unique transformative ability. After the terror attacks, many songs were banned, albums reworked, and tours postponed. Still, musicians, those wonderful angels on earth, united to create inspiring songs and raise hundreds of millions of dollars in relief money for survivors..

People look to artists for leadership, guidance, and solace during strife. As I have already said, but repeat for emphasis: the arts are not frivolous accessories; they are a deep human need, a necessity.

We owe a debt of gratitude to the many protectors of art who have come before us. During World War II, 348 brave souls from 14 nations, largely curators and professors, volunteered for service in the Monuments, Fine Arts, and Archives (MFAA) Section of Civil Affairs of the Western Allied Armies. Collectively, they confiscated tens of thousands of priceless works of art that had been looted by the Nazis and were in danger of being lost to the world. Among the artworks they confiscated were eight panels of one of the great masterpieces of fifteenth-century Europe, *The Adoration of the Mystic Lamb* by Hubert and Jan van Eyck. The works they restored and returned to their rightful owners included pieces by Botticelli, Rembrandt, Vermeer, Michelangelo, and Manet. Two Monuments Men sacrificed their lives to preserve the culture and history of European art.

Why would these people, primarily volunteers, risk everything to save artifacts instead of people? Because they understood. They knew the intrinsic value of these timeless masterpieces, which transcended the canvas and reflected the culture, religious tradition, and the rich history of European civilization. These works elevate our thinking and broaden our understanding of humanity.

Their work had faded from history until author Lynn H. Nicholas discovered the obituary of a female French spy, Jeanne Bohec, who was able to save sixty thousand works of art from Nazi looting. After ten years of researching these efforts, Nicholas shared her findings in her 1995 book, *The Rape of Europa,* which was followed by Robert Edsel's

2007 book, *The Monuments Men,* which became the 2014 film directed by George Clooney. Thanks to these writers and artists, this vital contribution to European art became known to the world. Art reflects life, reflecting art.

I have been blessed to live in Winston-Salem, North Carolina, where the arts have been celebrated and revered for most of my life. We have the University of North Carolina School of the Arts, the Winston-Salem Symphony, the Piedmont Opera, and more groups dedicated to the arts. Many incredible artists live among us. They enrich our lives and challenge our minds.

Every child should study music, whether or not they have an aptitude for it. If you study music, you will carry it with you for the rest of your life. You can still play an instrument long after losing the ability (for example) to play football, baseball, or basketball. And if you can't play, you can always appreciate it.

My first introduction to the arts was in the fourth grade, when I was in a little operetta. I remember having the realization that the arts were for me.

My family, too, cared about music. My dad had a beautiful voice. He and his brothers would sing when there was a Homecoming. We participated in our church choir. I had violin lessons, piano lessons, and voice lessons. I was a failure at all of them, and the irony of voice lessons was that I developed a paralyzed vocal cord as an adult, and now I sound like a frog! Though I was not destined to be a virtuoso, I learned focus and discipline, and I developed a great love of and appreciation for the arts through my exposure to music. One thing I do very well is applaud. I applaud talent, effort, and invention. They make my heart sing!

This is one of the reasons I love to applaud and open the minds of young people. They are the future thinkers and creators of our world. And, in my opinion, if there's one thing the world needs right now, it is artists.

Every period in history has unique triumphs and challenges, and we are living in an exciting time. A whole world of innovation and possibility awaits those who will open it and present it. That gives you a choice:

You can walk through your life blowing in the wind, full of fear and trepidation, asking yourself, "What am I doing here?" or you can choose to embrace this crazy time of unknowns and say, "I'm the next best thing. I don't know yet what that is, but I'm eager and excited to find out."

Art expands the mind and uplifts the spirit, which (I cannot emphasize enough) makes it necessary. It also dramatically influences society, instilling values, changing opinions, and translating experiences across space and time. In these extraordinary days, there is no more powerful way to communicate than through art. Now, coupled with technology, art has a global platform like never before.

In these unprecedented times, grassroots ideas, or even seeds of ideas, have infinite possibilities to grow, challenging and educating a global audience.

Art has always mobilized the world.

We have all seen the multifaceted media platforms and outlets on which people from diverse cultures of all ages communicate with each other via video, images, sounds, stories, and music. There has been a sweeping wave of change in communication; technology is evolving at lightning speed, and a new generation is leading the way.

Of course, there is fear. You are not alone if you wobble in the face of uncertainty.

If you are a young person starting in life, you may ask, "Where do I start? Where will I get work? We've survived a pandemic; will the world ever be the same?"

These are valid and reasonable questions. And the answers are genuinely unknown—except for the last one: "Will the world ever be the same?"

The answer is "no."

I have learned that we are all forever evolving but remain resilient. Who's to say our "new normal" doesn't mean an even brighter future? Like Mother before me, my glass is always half full. I see little value in focusing only on the doom and gloom in the world. Ask yourself what you can do to make it a better place. It doesn't have to be a huge event. You don't have to become rich or famous (though maybe you will), but it is important to consider: What will your contribution be?

George Bailey, the protagonist in *It's a Wonderful Life,* the beautiful 1946 Frank Capra film, was a hardworking banker who had sacrificed his dreams for others. Thinking his life had been worthless, he was contemplating suicide on Christmas Eve until his guardian angel appeared and showed him what an incredible impact George's life had had on his family and community. He had helped so many people without even knowing it.

If you have never experienced this momentous movie, I highly recommend it. The themes are timeless and still resonate today. It is a movie that asks us to consider our legacies.

What do you want your legacy to be? How can you count your time here? How can you make your mark on your community, family, and friends? Do what you can rather than focus on what you can't.

No one can profess to know what the future holds, but I assure you: You will find your way. You can look to art and artists for guidance. Throughout time, artists have forged distinctive paths, and yours will be a unique unfolding that will blossom in its own time and form.

Every journey has challenges, but I advise you to embrace them and use them as learning experiences. Don't just make lemonade; make a new kind of never-seen-before lemonade. There is a world of possibility and opportunity at your fingertips. Be proactive, daring, and true to yourself in our ever-changing magical world.

LESSON 3

MEET THEM WHERE THEY ARE

The mind is not a vessel to be filled, but a fire to be kindled.
—Plutarch

When I consider my legacy, I think about my fantastic, rewarding career as a high school English teacher. I've been asked how a teacher should balance the top, bottom, and middle of the class. In other words, "How do you teach the smart ones and the not-as-smart ones at the same time?"

I never thought of it that way. As a teacher, you try to work with each individual *where they are* and regret that, periodically, you have to grade them. Because a grade doesn't do justice to who the person is or what they've gone through outside that classroom. I think that's especially true with English. Science or math is more specific, but English is extensive. There are many facets to the English language. A student may not do very well in one part of the curriculum, perhaps because it doesn't interest them. But something else may strike them as important, and they think: "Wow!"

Occasionally, I would have a student who, for one reason or another, just tuned-out of school, life, and everything else and was hard to reach. But most young people are not like that. I could get to most students in some way. It was a matter of finding the right key. When I heard students talking about a TV program or a certain person, I made a mental note of it. Then I read about them or listened to their music so that I would know. When I was teaching in the '60s and '70s, I made myself listen to what I then considered some of the worst music I'd ever had to listen to! Some people may like very loud rock 'n roll music, but I was not among them!

I listened to that music anyway, because it's essential to meet people *where they are.* This applies not only to students but to all people. If you want to reach someone, discover their interests and what makes them tick.

I read the sports page, but not because I'm interested in sports—I do it because I'm interested in the people who are interested in sports. If I don't know what's going on in that world, that's one less opportunity I've given myself to connect with them. I've often said I read the headlines and articles so I can talk to my brothers. I don't read the *entire* sports page, but I read enough to know what my brothers are talking about and surprise them by commenting. And this applies even more to my students. I could walk into class on Monday morning and ask some of my boys, "What about those Braves?" And, of course, they would tell me all about it. Even if all I had seen was the headline, that was enough.

Meet them where they are.

My classroom had two walls with bulletin boards and low bookcases. I had lots of paperbound books. I'd buy them from Scholastic Books, which were inexpensive books students could read. Of course, this was back when people read real books. There were no Kindles or other electronic options then, but the principle still applies. I would encourage my students to use the school and public libraries, but I also had books in the room that they could use. I wanted to give them easy access to knowledge and help them experience the joy of discovering the gifts that reading a book has to offer.

I thought a lot about what to post on the bulletin boards. They were a unique opportunity to draw in my students and pique their interest. I read our local newspaper, and back then, frequent articles mentioned Reynolds High School, where I was teaching at the time—most of the articles were about sports, but there would be other things, too. I clipped out any article that mentioned Reynolds High School and placed it on the newspaper bulletin board. Usually, I highlighted "Reynolds High School" with a yellow highlighter. Many students I taught (and others I didn't teach, especially athletes), would come by the room and check out that board. I would attract them to the boards with the sports articles, but the surrounding bulletin boards were also essential. Once they were engaged with the articles about the school, I could expose them to a world beyond it.

I subscribe to *The New Yorker* and love its covers. I would put these attractive covers on an adjacent bulletin board and frequently post reviews of plays, movies, or music, or a cartoon that was particularly clever. Inevitably, something would catch their eye, and the students would migrate to that board.

I did a third board for many years, topped with a banner that read *Discover a Bigger World Beyond and Within Oneself.* I would put up other banners too: *Read, Travel, Create.* Under each of those areas, I'd put a picture I found in some magazine, maybe *The New Yorker, The Atlantic, Time,* or *Life* magazine. That way, I could change the pictures from semester to semester, year to year, but the idea of discovering a bigger world was an ongoing theme.

The students were such interesting people. They had inquisitive minds. If you can tap into a curious mind and inspire it to seek more knowledge about life, all sorts of possibilities emerge.

There was also room to do a board or two related to their studies. I might get a student or a group of students and ask them, "Is anybody interested in doing a Shakespeare or *Macbeth* board?" A board like that would be timely to what I was teaching. They volunteered because some loved to do artwork or design, and the board was a good creative outlet for them. When they had finished, they would proudly say, "Look what I did!"

Meet them where they are.

One of my former students, Scott Eagle, became an art teacher at East Carolina University and creates exciting and unusual art. I remember a piece he did on *Macbeth.* I put it up on the board, along with other related things, while my class was studying the play. Scott showed remarkable talent at a young age. Several years ago, his mural was displayed on the side of the American Embassy in China. Like a prized garden, talent needs to be nurtured and cared for in order for it to grow.

With students, an audience, or anyone you're trying to reach, you look for opportunities to get them all involved. You don't want anyone just sitting there, wasting space and time in their lives. Get them engaged. Once you engage them, it's like driving a Maserati. There is nothing in the world more satisfying and exhilarating. And all you have to do is: *meet them where they are.*

LESSON 4
FIND YOUR PASSION

Our deepest fear is not that we are inadequate. Our deepest fear is that we are powerful beyond measure. It is our light, not our darkness, that most frightens us. We ask ourselves, Who am I to be brilliant, gorgeous, talented, fabulous? Actually, who are you not to be? You are a child of God. Your playing small does not serve the world. There's nothing enlightened about shrinking so that other people won't feel insecure around you. We are all meant to shine, as children do. We were born to manifest the glory of God that is within us. It's not just in some of us; it's in everyone. And as we let our own light shine, we unconsciously give other people permission to do the same. As we're liberated from our own fear, our presence automatically liberates others.

—Marianne Williamson, *A Return to Love: Reflections on the Principles of A Course in Miracles*

What do you want to be when you grow up? Does this sound familiar? It is an age-old question that adults ask children. Some children square their shoulders and confidently answer, "I want to be a race car driver!" Or a firefighter, or a teacher, or a doctor, or, or . . . There are exceptions, but most five-year-olds change their minds many times before they land on their chosen career path. And rare is the child who doesn't look bewildered when put on the spot with that question.

A more interesting question is, "*Who* do you want to be when you grow up? Or, *who* do you want to be right now?"

When I ask this question, I am reminded that life is a gift. We all share this "ordinary" gift. But a gift is a precious commodity, not to be taken for granted. How do you want to use yours? What tenets in life are important to you? What type of person are you? What type of person do you *want* to be? Are you that person now, or is it something you aspire to? Philosophers have been pondering the meaning of life since humanity began. Unsurprisingly, they have yet to come up with one definitive answer; there is much to ponder.

Life is rich with blessings and full of promise. You are the architect of yours.

I remember a student quoting Doris A. Wright in her yearbook: "The future lies before you, like a field of fallen snow; Be careful how you tread it, for every step will show."

This raises a number of questions: Which steps do you want to show in your life? What is your passion? Do you have a passion? Are you feeling lost or confused because you don't know? Passion is an interesting thing. It can hit us between the eyes at an early age or, like a tiny flame, be fanned and nurtured into a raging inferno.

One can be passionate about many things: puppies, flowers, good conversation, a nice meal, music, dance, or a beautiful painting. As we fall into the routine of our daily lives, sometimes we forget to fan the flame of our passion. While passion can be like a flame, it can also be, as I have mentioned, like a garden. You sow the seeds, water the plants, tend the soil, and reap the rewards. However, if you neglect the soil, forget to water the seedlings, and allow the weeds to take over, your garden is lost . . . but only for a season. There is always a new spring full of new beginnings, opportunities, and passions. Some people never sow their seeds because they fear the seeds won't grow. I say, if the worst thing that can happen is a field full of weeds, what have you got to lose? Maybe the weeds will be beautiful and wild and exciting. After all, weeds are only weeds if you don't like them.

For example, morning glory, also known as bindweed, is a persistent, highly invasive weed, yet it is quite beautiful to many: it is a vine with lovely pink or white trumpet-shaped blooms. Left to its own devices, it can wrap itself around other plants and suffocate them, but many people love to grow it in their garden along with their other plants. A guiding hand and a caring touch can temper its aggressive behavior and nurture it to thrive and blossom into its full and glorious potential.

Beauty is in the eye of the beholder. You may consider your ideas and passions to be like weeds. They keep coming back, but they are not worth pursuing.

You might find yourself thinking, "Who would ever want to know what I think or feel or have to say?"

You will only know the answer once you tend your garden.

Weeds are also highly resilient. Have you ever noticed that even in places where you can't grow anything else, weeds somehow survive? And not just survive; they often thrive. They are nearly impossible to eradicate and can often grow in a wide range of soil and weather conditions. If you have ideas that (much like a beautiful weed) won't let you go, stir your passion, and make you curious, don't you owe it to yourself to let them grow? Maybe they are a little "out there" and wild, or maybe they are just timidly peeking their heads out of the soil and wondering what to do next. Why not water them and find out? At worst, you can discard them. At best, they will blossom into a gorgeous bouquet of fragrance and beauty. But won't you feel more alive for having pursued them and explored them?

As I have said and cannot emphasize enough, life is a gift not to be wasted. It is your gift. Be the architect you want to be. It's your house and your garden. Play in it and reap your rewards.

LESSON 5

MENTORSHIP

If I have seen further, it is by standing on the shoulders of giants.

—Sir Isaac Newton

I would be remiss if I didn't take a moment to discuss a critical part of any person's development: mentorship. Mentorship is extremely valuable to anyone's growth, but it is especially critical for a person who may not have a lot of support from their family circumstances.

Mentorship is a unique and valuable relationship between two individuals in which the more experienced and knowledgeable person supports, guides, and advises the other person. The "mentee" is typically less experienced in a particular area. Mentorship can be valuable in various contexts, including academic or professional situations, personal development, hobbies, or other interests. Its primary goal is to facilitate the mentee's growth and development. Mentors help their mentees navigate challenges, set goals, and achieve success by offering encouragement, constructive feedback, and practical insights. These relationships are not always formal. They can be structured or organic, depending on the situation and the needs or preferences of those involved.

For a mentoring relationship to be effective, mutual respect, active communication, and commitment to the mentee's growth and development must be mutual. It is an excellent opportunity for those seeking to enhance their skills or advance their careers or personal aspirations.

This book is a beautiful opportunity for me to pay it forward and acknowledge the influences of many incredible people who have helped shape my life. It is essential to recognize how crucial these individuals are. Sometimes, there is a perception in our society that no one person can make a difference, and yet one teacher who inspires someone can change the trajectory of their entire life.

I have been blessed to have had many teachers and mentors. Some were my parents' friends, many were teachers by profession, some were colleagues, some were friends, and some were my students. One is never too young or old to glean wisdom from anyone of any age or background.

Mother and Dad enjoyed the arts but were busy raising our family. Despite that, they managed to find the leisure time to take me to many local beautiful arts events. I was the first baby to come along whom the adults in their friend group could dote upon, so I got some extra-familial attention from birth! Each of their friends would periodically sign up to take me somewhere. None of them had families yet, so I had a community supporting me from the beginning. I am incredibly grateful for those people and the fabulous artistic experiences they orchestrated for me. They also became phenomenal adult role models. Their actions spoke louder than words; and even as a child, I could see what fine individuals they were.

I also had the best grade school music teacher. She encouraged us regardless of our level of innate talent. By nurturing me, she influenced the approach I took with all my own students, and I worked hard to emulate her style and inspire a new generation in my adult life. I have had marvelous teachers throughout my life, and I remember all of them. A good teacher is a natural mentor. You can't be a teacher and not live and breathe the role. It is more than a profession. It is a calling.

My teachers cultivated within us, their students, a sense of responsibility. When I was in the eighth and ninth grades, there were rare occasions when a teacher had to leave school or couldn't come to school at the last minute. Sometimes they were sick or had had an accident. If they needed somebody to take care of the elementary class, check the roll, and be sure everything was taken care of, they would call upon me. I was called several times during a year to fulfill a "teacher" role. I was honored to have been chosen and took this responsibility seriously. It honed my leadership skills and helped me grow as a person.

I went to school in the county, but there were four big high schools in the city of Winston-Salem: Reynolds, Gray, and Hanes for white students, and Atkins for black students. Yes, it was a very different time.

Thank goodness we have evolved somewhat as a culture since then. I taught at all four of those esteemed institutions in my career, which was fascinating. I would never have had such opportunities if not for the people who nurtured me along the way. In addition to the music teacher I have mentioned, I had two high school teachers who were very special to me, particularly my English teacher, Mrs. Newman. She taught twelfth grade, but I also had her for French and tenth grade English. She was the type of teacher we were all afraid of until she became our teacher. Then, once she started teaching us, it was so inspiring. She was a bit distant, but the best part of her teaching style was that she demanded a lot of us. She expected us to do well, whatever the task. She knew how to bring the best out of us.

I had another fine English teacher for eleventh grade, Mrs. Pratt. She was a force to be reckoned with, just like Mrs. Newman; these were strong women. But, as much as I loved Mrs. Pratt, Mrs. Newman was *extra* special. I would walk by her desk daily and see what books she was reading that were not our textbooks. That's where I learned about a lot of new authors. I remember one time she was reading a book by John Dos Passos. I would see her books in class, then go to the public library to get them to read on my own. I would never have had such a rich education if it hadn't been for Mrs. Newman.

Mrs. Newman also (interestingly enough) directed the junior and senior class plays. Her husband owned a gas and coal company but was very interested in technical theater. Our community theater, "The Little Theatre," still has the Paul Newman Award for Technical Aspects of Theater. No, not *that* Paul Newman: Mrs. Newman's husband.

The plays at our high school were outstanding because Mrs. Newman directed them, and she was a dynamo. Mr. Newman ensured we had the proper sets, lighting, and sound equipment. We didn't have a drama department, but Mrs. Newman was a one-woman drama department. It was a joy participating in several of those plays.

Later, when I was in college and it came time to do my student teaching, Dr. Elizabeth Welsh, another powerhouse and a significant influence on me and my career, assigned me to Mrs. Newman.

I remember saying, "Oh, Miss Newman,"—we called women

"Miss" in the South regardless of marital status— "I'm so afraid they won't let me come and teach with you when they find out you were my teacher, friend, and mentor. They'll send me to someone else."

She said, "Oh, my dear, we shan't tell them, shall we?" She was something.

I said, "Oh no! I'm not going to say a word!"

Later, when I was thirty-four, I had the honor and privilege of returning to North Forsyth High School as a teacher with Mrs. Newman as the English department chair. It was glorious!

Six or eight months after Mrs. Newman passed away, I received a box in the mail through her attorney. There were diamond and amethyst rings and beads, jade and amber carvings, a small lusterware picture, and a poem she had written. There was also a beautiful photo of her, which I treasure. I was overwhelmed! Imagine receiving a package in the mail and discovering a small inheritance upon opening it! I knew she had passed, but it had been some time since we had spoken, and this was the last thing I would ever have expected. What an honor and a priceless gift to be cherished. And I am forever amazed that it was unceremoniously sent in a plain box through the mail by an attorney!

For my postsecondary education, I studied at Salem College. It has a charmingly beautiful little campus in the heart of Old Salem. It's still an active private college, an excellent institution for higher learning, and it's still an all-women's school. There are a few male graduate students, especially in music—a man beyond college age with a unique talent or ability could study at Salem College. A couple of exceptional older students were also there under the GI Bill. Salem now has a highly gifted professor on the faculty, Dr. Barbara Lister-Sink. She developed a unique technique to help pianists who have injured themselves (whether because of their playing or for another reason), and she uses her method to facilitate their recovery.

Like the few male students there, I was also a mature student at Salem—not by design, but by circumstance. For a while I took a short break from mentors and mentorship, because of developments in my personal life.

In 1953, I married Bob Carswell, my first husband. On the day of our wedding rehearsal, Bob received his draft notice. We married, and then he was sent to basic training and EMP, a military police school in Georgia. He was a private in the army. When he finished both of those things, he was sent to Oklahoma. While he was in basic training, I studied. I took my first-semester junior year exams at Salem and then moved to Oklahoma in January. Late that following summer, he was transferred to Germany.

He worked as a clerk typist at the battalion's headquarters. When he finished that, I went over as a tourist because they didn't send wives of privates to join their husbands. We lived with a German family near his assigned post. I did not work when I was there. I hadn't finished school yet. I took time off from studying for two years. Oh, we had a great time!

When I returned in 1956, about a week before school started, I saw another mentor, Dean Ivy Hickson, in Salem. I walked into her office and said, "Dr. Hickson, school starts in a week. Am I too late to re-enroll?"

I remember how she got up and came around that big desk with her arms out. And she said, "Oh my dear, of course you can enroll."

She hugged me and said, "So many tell me they will return, and they don't. Of course, you can come back."

It was great. I am so fortunate to have been welcomed back with open arms at such a late date, well beyond the enrollment deadline. Because of Dr. Hickson's mentorship and generous leniency, I received a top-notch education from the most encouraging and talented professors.

My most demanding English professor was Miss Jess Byrd. I don't care how much you studied or how well prepared you were for class; it was never enough. She was so tough. Many of us went into that class trembling with fear because we knew we'd done everything we could to prepare, but we also knew that wouldn't be enough. She pushed us to be better, and better we became! She was amazing.

Salem College gave me the foundation for a lifelong career and passion as an educator. I finished my schooling in the middle of the year. I majored in English and history with a minor in psychology.

After getting married and spending two years in Europe, I was two years older than my classmates. By then, I had done all my student teaching, so in January, the middle of the school year, I had everything finished. One day, Dr. Elizabeth Welsh, a remarkable professor and incredible mentor, dropped a note on my desk and unceremoniously left the room. The note said: "Miss Carswell (remember, back then you were "Miss" so-and-so), call this number after class."

There was no name on it, just a phone number. And I thought, "If Dr. Elizabeth Welsh said call this number, oh my gosh, I'd better call the number!"

So, after class was over, I called. It was the office of Dr. William Self, the associate superintendent of Winston-Salem City Schools. I told the secretary I was from Salem College, and Dr. Welsh had told me to call.

"Oh yes," she said, and asked if I could meet with Dr. Self that afternoon. At that time the administrative office for the city schools was close to Old Salem and Salem College.

I replied, "Oh, yes, indeed."

And so I went! I'd never met Dr. Self, but he was very friendly and said, "I understand you want to teach English."

"Yes." I replied tentatively.

He said, "There's a teacher at Gray High School who has to resign because her husband has been transferred to a different city for his job, and they're expecting their first child. She will be leaving, so we must hire an English teacher for that position. Would you have time for me to take you over to the school so you can meet the chair of the English Department and perhaps the principal?"

And I said, "Oh, yes, sir!"

A job!

I remember when we got to his car, he apologized for the mess. He looked abashed and muttered, "I didn't know I was going to take somebody in the car."

We laughed about that, and he drove me to the school. There I met Miss Mozell Stephenson. She was the chair of the English department at Gray High School, and her sister was the chair of the English department at Reynolds High School. These two sisters, like the other formidable female teachers and mentors I've mentioned, were powerful women.

I briefly met the principal after meeting with Miss Stephenson, who was very friendly. Before we went over to Gray High School, Dr. Self said, "Come with me." He took me to meet the superintendent, Dr. Greg Philips. Dr. Philips later became the superintendent of public education for the State of North Carolina.

When that was over, Dr. Self dropped me back at Salem College, where I had left my car.

He said, "Of course, we need to interview some other applicants, but I will be in touch."

As the associate superintendent, though, he was not in charge of personnel. So, I met the associate superintendent and the superintendent. I still had not met anybody in personnel or HR, but a couple of days later, Dr. Self called and said, "You have a position at Gray High School."

And here I was, *GREEN!*

My husband was still in school, so for me to get a job was excellent. He had a part-time job with the post office, which was fabulous, but he would finish at the end of that year, so my getting a job was a big deal. I didn't even have to apply—I just followed Dr. Welsh's command to "Call this number!"

Dr. Welsh later became one of my neighbors, and she would say, "Now, Phyllis, please call me Elizabeth." I gulped every time, but eventually, I was able to do so.

Later, I was in an educator group with my mentor and the academic dean of Salem College, Dr. Ivy Hickson, the same woman who had hugged me and welcomed me back to Salem without hesitation. She taught Latin and Greek. I never took those courses, but I was extremely grateful that she embraced my desire to continue my education, and I revered her for her intelligence and accomplishments. Talk about a formidable person! Because she was the academic dean, everybody knew her. She was just incredible. After I graduated, I joined Gray High School.

Like Dr. Welsh, Dr. Hickson would say, "Oh, Phyllis, please, call me Ivy." Well, I never could call her by her first name. That was just too much! These were two remarkable women and exemplary mentors, Elizabeth Welsh and Ivy Hickson.

One of the things I loved about the mentorships and associations I made while a student at Salem College was that we students were encouraged to ask questions and voice our opinions about the subject matter we were studying. This type of dialogue and sharing of ideas engages the mind, helps expand one's thinking, and elevates learning. We didn't just regurgitate information for testing; we actively *pondered* and made our own conclusions. This was common practice at Salem.

I became incredibly grateful for this encouraging and open environment when, after Salem College, I attended Wake Forest University—another fine and well-respected educational institution in Winston-Salem. My courses there were co-ed, but I was the only woman in class who ever asked a question or offered an opinion. Co-ed classes were largely male-dominated, but I would speak up. The professors were often men as well. Frequently, some of the other female students and I would have coffee after class. We would sit around talking, and they were bright—sharper and more intelligent than I was. But they never said a word in class. Sometimes, we'd talk about what we'd just been discussing in class, and they would have so many beautiful things to say.

I'd ask, "Why didn't you say that in class?"

They'd reply, "Well, the guys..."

And I'd tell them, "Friends, I am so delighted I went to a women's college that expected us to speak up, question, challenge, and be leaders, not sit around deferring to others!" That was the power of a Salem College education, and I am forever grateful to every professor who taught us critical thinking and encouraged us to think independently.

The co-eds were so intelligent. They were afraid the boys would think they were too bright. I didn't have any problems with speaking up because I was married, but they were more worried about their dating prospects than they were about knowledge.

Though it was a different experience from Salem, I enjoyed my classes at Wake. Sometimes I would take twenty-one or twenty-four hours of courses in a semester. I would carry an extra load or two because there were so many classes I wanted to take in so little time! I didn't have time to take political science in the regular semesters, so one summer, I went up to Wake and took four political sciences courses. When I went to sign up for one of them, the registering professor could see that I had not taken the prerequisite for this geopolitics course. By then, I'd graduated from Salem and had taught for maybe half a year.

He looked up and said, "Are you at least a junior?"

And I said, "Yes, sir, several years ago."

He laughed and said, "Okay," and signed me up.

I loved those courses. My favorite professor (and one I would consider a mentor) was Dr. Milner. After he retired, he was named Professor Emeritus of the School of Education at Wake Forest. He was a prince of a human being. He and his wife, Lucy, started the Governor's School for talented high school juniors and seniors in North Carolina.

Students could be invited to participate in the North Carolina Governor's School in two ways: one was to have a talent in the arts, and the other was to have talent in a subject like math, English, or chemistry. High school juniors and seniors invited to participate in this summer program were exceptionally talented, bright students in some aspects. Dr. Milner and his wife, Lucy, were outstanding pedagogues and knew how to work with those students.

I taught and mentored many talented students who went to Governor's School, and I also had numerous equally talented students who didn't go, but who fit all the criteria.

I took various courses with Dr. Milner. One of his specialties was teaching or engaging intelligent students. He taught us all sorts of techniques to get students involved. You don't want students just *sitting there,* taking up space and wasting time in their lives. It was imperative to get them engaged. Once you engage them, the sky is the limit as to what they can do. It is exciting to see them unleash their potential.

Five times a day, I had a room full of talented, bright students—that's five rooms full. My courses with Dr. Milner gave me an arsenal of ideas for inspiring them. Dr. Milner was excellent at knowing, suggesting, and discussing ideas about working with those students—and he was just delightful as a friend and mentor.

I have been incredibly blessed to have had such exceptional role models and mentors. Having a guiding hand or a voice of encouragement changes a person's life. If you find a mentor in your life to help shape your experience, consider yourself fortunate. Sometimes, it can be an informal relationship with someone who influences your thinking or opens your mind to possibilities.

I have a former student who, to everyone's surprise, became a dentist. Everyone was convinced he would study something in the arts. When asked about it, he said his orthodontist made a big impression on him when he was a tween. One never knows where positive influences might come from. Keep your eyes open to find those people in your life. They make all the difference. My journey has been enriched by so many who taught me so much.

Besides my time at Salem and Wake Forest, I was also fortunate to be affiliated with another outstanding educational organization: the University of North Carolina School of the Arts. Uniquely for a conservatory, the School of the Arts is home to both high school and university students. It was the first state-supported conservatory in the United States, so it's a part of our university system, and students can pursue bachelor of fine arts or master of fine arts degrees in drama, dance, design and production, music, or filmmaking. At the same time, high school students can enroll—students in music and dance can be as young as thirteen or fourteen or in ninth grade; those in visual arts—drawing, painting, sculpture—must be juniors or seniors; and those in drama must be seniors. The school takes about forty high school juniors and seniors in visual arts and about twenty-five in drama. Most of them are from North Carolina.

For those high school students, a group called the Associates at the School of the Arts had a volunteer mentor program. Each volunteer was cleared through a background check for security and safety reasons. Once you were accepted as a mentor, you could be the host for a high school student. They lived on campus, but you would do things with your mentee, like take them out to dinner, or get them to a dentist or the airport. Or you could take them to cultural events like the symphony—if they had time—because they have worked so hard.

So, when I retired from teaching in 1993, I signed up for that program. Every year, they asked, "Would you rather have a boy, girl, US citizen, citizen of a foreign country, student of ballet, music, etc.?"

I would just say, "Whatever you need. Whoever needs somebody."

I would have one student each year, so I ended up with several dancers, a violinist, and some visual artists. My mentees were from all over—Saratoga, in upstate New York; St. Louis; Phoenix; San Francisco; Connecticut; Oak Island and Bald Head Island, North Carolina. One summer, Angela lived with me. She had a part-time job at Camino Coffee Shop and Bakery and was dating someone she would eventually marry. She wanted to stay in Winston-Salem that summer, and since I'd met her parents and everything, I agreed to let her stay with me. Only one of my mentees was from outside the continental United States—Diego, from Puerto Rico. His mother was a doctor there, and she came during the year and stayed with me. Then, when she came for his high school graduation, I was in Europe, but she stayed in my house. I gave my key to my next-door neighbor, and Diego's mother picked it up that weekend when she came for Diego's graduation.

Many of my mentees kept in touch. I have heard from Angela, who lives in Florida now. I've lost touch with Diego. After his parents divorced, his mother lived in Puerto Rico and his father lived in Mexico City.

The program was comforting for parents. They felt safer knowing that an adult was looking after their child. It gave them peace of mind to know that there were also volunteers in town who supported the school in addition to the school and the people there. After COVID-19 and due to worries about lawsuits and liability, the school has decided not to continue that program.

It was an excellent program, though. I met some extraordinary and talented young people. When you give, you get back in unexpected ways. Mentorship is a reciprocal, enriching relationship. I highly recommend it to anyone who wants to become a mentor. There is no prerequisite; you just need to care about the well-being and growth of others.

There are many famous examples of mentorship. A great example of a successful mentorship is the symbiotic relationship between the late Maya Angelou and Oprah Winfrey, which was second to none. Angelou was an acclaimed poet and author who had great insights into the human condition. It will behoove you to read her work. She was also a dear friend, mentor, and confidant to Oprah, who speaks fondly of Angelou's influence in shaping her personal and professional growth.

Maya Angelou extended profound wisdom and unwavering support to Oprah. Their relationship grew into a friendship that transcended mentorship. Angelou urged Oprah to embrace her authentic self and remain true to her core beliefs and values. Angelou's wisdom resonated deeply with Oprah and encouraged her to be bravely transparent and genuine in her public persona. Angelou's emphasis on authenticity emboldened Oprah to trust her instincts and to cultivate a high level of integrity in all aspects of her life.

Angelou drew from her experience and knowledge of the challenges of pioneering new pathways and breaking barriers as a black woman in the arts. She steadfastly advised Oprah, offering treasured insights when she was navigating the intricacies of the media industry. Whether aiding in career decisions or providing encouragement during challenging times, Angelou's mentorship gave Oprah a perpetual source of support and direction. And Angelou's resilience and grace in the face of adversity along her journey set a potent example for Oprah. Angelou overcame many extremely devastating challenges in her life, and she found beauty and meaning in these experiences. Oprah was inspired to confront her challenges with similar resilience, courage, and determination. Angelou's guiding hand empowered her to persevere in pursuit of her dreams.

Even a person destined to become a media mogul and generous philanthropist needs guidance and support. One might argue that successful people would never have attained such greatness in their chosen path had it not been for the shoulders they stood upon and the people who held them up. Angelou's guidance in helping to shape Oprah's personal and professional growth has left an indelible mark on both of their lives and legacies.

I cannot stress enough the importance of mentorship. Just having one person's encouragement and wisdom can be life-changing. And what a gift it is for the mentor to watch their mentee blossom! Making a meaningful impact on a person's life brings a beautiful sense of fulfillment. From my teaching experience, I can tell you that witnessing a mentee's growth and development brings a profound sense of satisfaction. What could be more rewarding than the knowledge you have contributed to shaping the lives of the next generation?

For the mentee, mentorship serves as a beacon illuminating a path toward success. The feeling of being supported and guided by a steady hand as one navigates seemingly daunting challenges is often the difference between success and failure. Knowing that someone believes in you and takes the time and care to aid your development is a powerful motivator. Being part of a team, rather than a lone light in the dark, empowers people beyond measure.

There are rewards for the mentor, too. Mentors are given the gift of reflecting on their experiences and achievements while gaining fresh perspectives and insights. They deepen their understanding of their field and hone their leadership skills. Being a mentor enriches one's sense of purpose and fulfillment. Fostering a mentee's personal and professional advancement enriches the mentor's own journey and growth. Like Maya Angelou and Oprah Winfrey, mentoring relationships often evolve into enduring friendships, potentially opening doors to new opportunities and collaborations.

For one person to simply say "I believe in you" is everything. People can move mountains when they have a strong foundation holding them up. One person who takes the time to pass on valuable knowledge and experience can change the world, one inquiring mind at a time.

I am forever grateful to the many mentors who have guided me. They have shaped me into the person I am today. So many opportunities came to me because of their nurturing hands. What a remarkable blessing they have been in my life. Don't forget that you can be that blessing in someone else's life. Maybe you're already that person and haven't yet realized it. I encourage you to take inventory of the people who have held you up, and, once you have finished thanking your lucky stars for them, turn your beacon outward and shine a light on someone else's path.

LESSON 6

THE POWER OF BOOKS

"The world is full of magic things, patiently waiting for our senses to grow sharper."
—William Butler Yeats

I love books. I love the look of them, the feel of them, the smell of them. It's impossible to pick a favorite. Once I've enjoyed one, I read everything that the author has written. I never could resist when I would run across a good book in my travels. I have accumulated quite a collection over the years. I found a set of hard-covered Shakespearean miniatures in the Lake Country in England in a little shop. They were so cute. They're not to be read, but they are just darling. I found a wonderful collection in Covent Garden—Rudyard Kipling, Robert Burns, Alfred, Lord Tennyson, Robert Browning, William Wordsworth, Lord Byron, Percy Bysshe Shelley, and John Keats. My favorite poet is the Irish poet William Butler Yeats. I love so many authors and poets.

My collection is also rich with gifts from friends. One of my sweet former students, Jorge Soccolich from Venezuela, sent me *The Man Without a Country*. He now lives in Texas.

I have a lovely copy of *Dream Children and Other Essays* with the inscription "To Phyllis from Jane Rae, Christmas 1983." Jane majored in biology with a minor in English and came to Reynolds to teach both. She and I took a group to London on spring break. Jane began taking her own groups after that. She and her husband graduated from Wake Forest, and after they moved to Delaware, they would come back for Homecoming, and we would always get together. I haven't seen her in years, but I think of her every time I look at that book.

Good books are like good friends. They can be out of sight, but you know where they are there when needed.

Books can expand the mind, reshape opinions, and deepen one's understanding of the world. Through books, a reader can access the thoughts of great minds, explore diverse perspectives, and dive into rich narratives that stretch beyond the limits of everyday experience. Whether through fiction or nonfiction, literature can introduce us to new ideas, change our views on important issues, and cultivate a sense of connection to humanity that transcends borders. Books provide a unique portal through which readers can broaden their intellectual and emotional horizons, becoming more thoughtful, empathetic, and well-informed.

For example, reading can introduce a person to worlds and viewpoints they may never encounter otherwise. Whether it's a novel set in a distant land or a historical account of an unfamiliar era, reading encourages an open mind. A novel that portrays life in a different part of the world can instill understanding and empathy, as readers see life through the characters' eyes. Have you ever read a book set in a town or country you've never visited but now feel connected to? Books can change your perspective in that way.

Books also provide a sense of immersion that allows readers to experience living with different customs, values, and challenges, thereby challenging assumptions and broadening outlook. They trouble and expand readers' opinions on social, political, and philosophical issues. A book presenting a well-researched argument or a moving personal story can lead readers to reevaluate their beliefs. Reading about environmental challenges or social justice issues through firsthand accounts or expert analyses often gives readers new insights and a sense of urgency that may inspire them to take action or adopt new perspectives. In this way, books catalyze personal growth, encouraging readers to question, reflect, and adapt their views in light of new information.

When you engage with a story, you temporarily set aside your identity and immerse yourself in the characters' lives. This process of imagining the thoughts and feelings of others stimulates emotional intelligence. In novels, characters often face complex moral dilemmas, difficult emotions, and personal growth, which can teach readers about the nuances of human experience. Reading about characters who deal with loss, struggle with identity, or navigate relationships provides a deeper understanding of these universal experiences.

This empathy extends beyond fictional characters to real-world issues. Books about historical events, social justice, or cultural traditions help readers better appreciate the struggles, achievements, and values of people from various backgrounds. A deepened sense of caring gives one a feeling of shared humanity and leads readers to appreciate the diversity of the human experience. This understanding builds a stronger community and encourages people to be more compassionate and thoughtful.

Uniquely and distinctively, fiction and poetry ignite the imagination in ways few other mediums can. They invite readers to envision worlds beyond their immediate reality, often filled with fantastical settings, intricate plots, and rich symbolism. Visualizing encourages creative thinking, allowing readers to approach problems and ideas with fresh perspectives. Science fiction and fantasy books often explore hypothetical societies or technologies that inspire readers to think about the future and its possibilities.

For instance, a novel examining the search for meaning can resonate with readers facing similar questions, inspiring them to consider what truly matters in their lives. This process of reflection can lead to a more authentic and fulfilling life as readers align their actions with their evolving self-awareness.

What an essential source of knowledge books are!

The knowledge found in books—from history and science to philosophy and art—not only makes readers well-rounded but also fuels their curiosity. The more people read, the more questions they come up with, leading them to explore new topics and seek further information. This intellectual curiosity keeps the mind active, promoting lifelong learning and personal enrichment. A well-read person is often better equipped to engage in meaningful conversations and contribute valuable insights to discussions on a wide range of topics.

Indeed, books have clearly had a lasting impact on the students I have taught. One of my former students, Dan Dodson, lives in New Jersey and has done well in his career. He's very sharp. His mother was a music teacher in Winston-Salem. He lives with his wonderful wife and darling son who is about twelve, a tennis player. I am always interested to read Dan's posts on Facebook, as he has a thoughtful perspective. He surprised me on my 92nd birthday by posting the most beautiful birthday wishes on my page. I was not surprised that he wished me a happy birthday but what he said was profound:

> "Wishing you a happy birthday. I know you've heard it from many former students, BUT I'll repeat it, you were my most impactful teacher.
>
> There's always been a notion in my mind that people could create something lasting through their words. I think about Shakespeare, Blake, Longfellow, Hawthorne, Waldon, Swift, Cummings, Bronte and Barnhardt [His classmate and author, about whom I've spoken in this book] with an eye towards what they are really saying about the human condition. I want that kind of high school American and English literature experience for my son. To think that it's something I still think about 45 years later is pretty amazing."

As Dan's message indicates, books (whether fiction or nonfiction) serve as windows to the world and mirrors for self-reflection, offering tools to better understand ourselves and the world around us. In a world that often demands quick answers and instant gratification, the enduring power of books lies in their ability to slow us down, make us think deeply, and ultimately change how we see ourselves and others. I have appreciated these benefits of reading ever since I was young.

When I was a child, it was the storytelling that drew me to books. I love a good story for the pure pleasure of that story. I love fiction. I was introduced to the classics in the classroom. I was fortunate to have wonderful teachers throughout my growing years. I remember them all amazingly well. I also have lots of curiosity and books satisfy that curiosity. I wanted to *know.* I *still* want to know.

I read to satisfy the questions that are always stirring in my mind.

"What's that?"

Or

"What is that doing?"

"Why is this *this* way, or how did *that* happen?"

Those answers come from both fiction and nonfiction. Good fiction is about life. Nonfiction is also about life.

Expanding one's mind through reading has far-reaching benefits: enhancing cognitive abilities, building resilience, and encouraging kindness and cultural appreciation. As our world becomes increasingly interconnected, complex challenges demand innovative solutions. Broadening one's intellectual and emotional horizons is not just beneficial but essential. Learning keeps the brain agile, helping it develop new neural connections and enhancing critical thinking skills. I have a very specific routine to help keep my mind open: I begin each day with a cup of coffee and the *New York Times* crossword puzzle, followed by a game of Sudoku.

People who actively engage in continuous learning often experience slower cognitive decline as they age. Learning new skills and ideas promotes mental sharpness. People who read widely, take up new hobbies, or engage in intellectual challenges (sometimes as simple as Sudoku and a crossword puzzle) often display greater adaptability and problem-solving abilities.

Continuing to learn and grow also contributes to improved decision-making. Reading deepens and broadens perspectives, equipping people to analyze situations from different angles, consider alternative solutions, and make informed choices. This capacity to approach problems with a well-rounded perspective is invaluable in personal and professional settings, where sound decision-making can lead to more significant achievements and satisfaction.

Resilience is *essential* to navigating life's ups and downs, and exposing oneself to different viewpoints, challenges, and experiences teaches one to manage uncertainty and bounce back from setbacks. Those who have studied diverse historical events or philosophical concepts often possess a broader context for interpreting their struggles. They recognize that hardship is a shared human experience. This awareness creates a mindset geared toward growth and perseverance, making it easier to face difficult situations with composure.

Adaptability is another benefit, particularly in a rapidly changing world where new technologies, social norms, and industries emerge quickly. Those who have gained a broad understanding of the world tend to be more flexible, open to change, and capable of evolving with shifting environments. This adaptability is a significant advantage in the modern workforce, where companies increasingly value employees who can learn, unlearn, and relearn as the world progresses.

Reading also enhances our acceptance and understanding of the diversity of the world around us. Exposure to different cultures, lifestyles, and ideologies deepens one's understanding of the human experience and creates a greater appreciation for diversity. Learning about others' backgrounds makes people more accepting of differences and compassionate toward those around them.

Empathy is the critical building block for creating meaningful relationships, promoting social harmony, and resolving conflicts with mutual respect. Reading literature from various cultures or studying foreign languages can enhance understanding of global perspectives and create a sense of shared humanity. This cultural appreciation enriches one's life and contributes to a more inclusive society, and by recognizing the value of varying viewpoints, people can work together more effectively, bridging cultural divides and collaborating on global challenges, such as climate change, poverty, and health care.

Exposure to new ideas and experiences through reading also often stimulates creative thinking, enabling individuals to connect seemingly unrelated concepts in fresh and imaginative ways. This cross-pollination of ideas has fueled some of history's most groundbreaking inventions and artistic achievements. Many scientists, writers, and artists have drawn inspiration from fields outside their own, resulting in novel insights and works that have reshaped society.

Creativity is a highly sought-after skill as companies seek innovative solutions to stay competitive. Those who have broadened their minds by exploring different disciplines and perspectives are more likely to approach problems with a unique viewpoint and suggest innovative solutions. The ability to think outside the box can set individuals apart, driving success and contributing to progress in their fields. That presents a strong case for being well-read and well-informed.

A great example of this is a highly intelligent student I taught named Karl Pfefferkorn. He was extremely inquisitive and exceptionally bright. He questioned *everything!* That would lead to lively discussions in the classroom. When we were studying a book, he would inspire others to ask questions. He would stimulate great conversation, because he did not take anything at face value.

I embraced teaching him. He was a challenge in all the best ways. I loved it, because in order for him to question, he had to be paying attention. He had to have read; he had to have heard what I said. To me that's what makes a class wonderful. You don't want a room full of quiet little mice. Inevitably, students understand the material better when there is discussion. Those questioning students were among my favorites. I loved that they put me through my paces. I had to bring my "A game" to the classroom!

Invariably a book, any book, would resonate with some and not with others. Or it might not be a book. It might be an individual poem or something that came up in discussion as a result of talking about a particular passage or concept.

I would ask, "Is there anything in this book written in 1927 (or 1843, or whatever) that you or I or any of us can relate to in today's world?"

Someone would make a suggestion and there would be students who would agree with whatever was said.

Then, I could count on Karl if he was in that class to respond: "I disagree!"

He would have a different slant on it. He would question what the writer was saying and whether or not there was any relevance. As I said, he questioned absolutely everything, which was great because that just stirred the pot; and the more the pot was stirred, the more interesting things would bubble up.

In what seemed like no time at all, the bell would ring, and class would be over! None of the students had been bored because there had been a lively and insightful discussion! Some people don't like to rock the boat, but I always admire people who have an opinion... and I mean a real opinion. It can be a dissenting opinion, but these people don't care. And they can sway a room. As a student, especially back in high school, I wouldn't question or rock the boat. As a college student—and, as I have said, I thank Salem for this—I was encouraged to speak up.

As an example of how a single text can change a life: I used to include T. S. Elliot in my curriculum whether I was teaching American Literature or British Literature (because he was a citizen of both countries). I would *always* include the poem, *The Love Song of J. Alfred Prufrock.*

There are a lot of quotable lines in it. J. Alfred Prufrock was afraid to take a chance:

"Do I dare to eat a peach?"

When we studied that poem, I always said to my students, "Don't you *dare* be afraid to take a risk. Don't be a J. Alfred Prufrock!"

I have another great example of how themes from a work like *The Love Song of J. Alfred Prufrock* can influence substantial life choices, and I have so many examples of former students who have learned valuable life lessons from literature, it is a pity to omit any of them. One of my former students, Connie Irving, now lives in Israel. I taught her as a junior, and then she went to Choate Rosemary Hall, a prep school in the Northeast. Most of those who attend that school go on to an Ivy League school. She received a big scholarship to Carnegie Mellon but came back to North Carolina after a year.

She wrote to me and said, "Mrs. Dunning, I do not like Carnegie Mellon. They want to put me in a particular track, but what I want is a very broad, strong liberal arts education. So, I am going to transfer to Guilford College."

I know Guilford well. My brothers Don and Rick, my first husband Bob, my nephews Don, Jr. and Scott, and a lot of my friends attended Guilford College. It's a Quaker school with a fine reputation. I always appreciated that she chose the school that would give her the education she desired over the prestige of a better-known school. She was definitely NOT a J. Alfred Prufrock!

Connie was a brilliant writer, who majored in philosophy and history, went to Israel, married a rabbi, and now has children and grandchildren. Her Hebrew name is the equivalent of Hannah, spelled (with Hebrew letters) C-H-I-A-N-A. She continued to write and also became a nurse.

Connie was a piece of work! I can see her now, sitting in class. One day, we were reading "To a Waterfowl," by William Cullen Bryant. Connie was taking notes with her textbook and notebook out on the desk. On her lap under the desk, she had another book open. She was very engaged in our discussion, asking questions and commenting on things. But she was also, simultaneously, reading her chosen book on her lap.

She dropped a page from her notebook on my desk at the end of the class and went out the door. She had written a poem, "To a Water*foul*." F-O-U-L. It was a wonderful environmental poem about the need for clear, fresh water. She had used Bryant's stanza structure, rhyme scheme, and meter to write this satire. Brilliant. *Brilliant!* That's what she was doing as she was taking notes, listening, participating in the discussion, and reading some other book simultaneously. Talk about multitasking! She could do it all!

When I saw students doing things like reading under their desks or successfully multitasking, I often didn't say anything because I used to do the same thing as a student!

I would never discourage a student's passion for books. But sometimes, just for kicks, if I saw them sometime after class, I would say, "What was that other book you had in your lap reading today? Was it good?"

They'd say, "You saw me do that?!"

I'd say, "I have eyes on the back of my head!"

Expanding the mind is a journey, not a destination. The ripple effects of this growth contribute to a more knowledgeable, understanding, and dynamic world where people are empowered to reach their potential and work collaboratively to address global challenges. Expanding one's mind is about learning and living a life of purpose, connection, and discovery, and books (indeed, all literature) can allow us to tap into a well-lived life and flourish.

LESSON 7

BOOK CLUB

Not surprisingly, I am a passionate member of my local book club. I don't have room to host a meeting at home, so I co-host either at somebody's house or in a larger venue like Forsyth Country Club or Old Town Country Club. Sometimes we'll meet at one of the clubs and invite guests to come. There are fourteen club members, so we might have thirty or forty people when we invite guests. Our members know many good readers who like attending our events.

We often host speakers at these events. Dr. Ed Wilson used to come and speak annually. He was provost at Wake Forest University and professor of Romantic poetry. He would select the book, always a classic, for February and come discuss it with us. Most of us were reading whatever the book was for the second or third time in our lives. Ed Wilson was a compelling speaker, known as the best in Winston-Salem, and he was also the most wonderful person. His wife is a writer, and she's fantastic, too. We eventually made Dr. Wilson an honorary member of our book club.

When it was time to sign up for courses at Wake Forest, students—even those whose main interest was not literature—would line up to try to get into Dr. Wilson's class. He was the most beloved professor at Wake Forest for over fifty years; generations of students loved his courses. Emily Wilson (Ed's wife) writes both poetry and prose, and created booklets of some of his favorite poems. What a wonderful keepsake for all!

He retired from speaking at our book club when he reached about ninety-four years of age, though he lived to be a hundred. We then invited Phil Archer, the Deputy Director of Reynolda House Museum, to come and speak. He is also beloved and was one of Ed's protégés at Wake Forest. We asked Phil to do what Ed used to do—choose the book, then review and talk about it.

Phil wanted us to reread American bookseller and publisher Sylvia

Beach's book, *Shakespeare and Company,* a memoir about her bookstore of the same name in Paris. It includes her reminiscences of Gertrude Stein, Ernest Hemingway, F. Scott Fitzgerald, and James Joyce. She knew them all. When nobody else would publish Joyce, Beach did. I had read the book years before, having frequented her bookstore in Paris. The shop has since become a tourist attraction and is, unfortunately, not like it used to be when I first visited in the 1950s.

I reread *Shakespeare and Company* for this occasion. Phil came and talked with us about the book, the bookstore, and the writers of the time (including the ones I have just mentioned: Hemingway, Fitzgerald, Stein and, of course, James Joyce). Then, Phil stood up and quoted a passage from James Joyce's *Finnegans Wake* from memory. He concluded by giving each of us a copy of this quote—a full typewritten page.

I like James Joyce and sometimes read stories from *Dubliners* with my students. Some would read *A Portrait of the Artist as a Young Man,* which I've read several times. And though I've never had any students read *Ulysses,* I have read it multiple times.

I've tried to read *Finnegans Wake* in the past, and I have failed every time. Joyce intentionally made the book obscure, even creating his own language for it—it might as well have been written in Sanskrit or Greek! I can make neither heads nor tails of it! *Portrait of the Artist* and *Ulysses,* William Faulkner, stream-of-consciousness writing—these are challenges. Finnegans Wake, however, is in a league of its own. Yet Phil Archer not only read it (and can read it) but *memorized and recited it* beautifully. We were all astounded!

A knowledgeable person who shares their wisdom and insights can bring material to life, making the learning potential profound. Listening to people like Phil and Ed, both with the ability to captivate their audiences, is a true privilege. Their accumulated expertise and experience offer insights from years, sometimes decades, of learning in a distilled form. How fortunate we have been to have each of them enrich our experiences with their personal stories, reflections, and hard-earned lessons. And the choice of reading material gives us new vantage points, enhancing our critical thinking skills and inspiring us.

One of the most incredible benefits of reading literature and sharing the experience with a learned person is that they can introduce us to new perspectives and ways of thinking. Not only do they help us decode insightful literature, they often challenge us to question our assumptions, expand our viewpoints, and approach problems creatively. A learned person may share an insight that reframes how we see an issue, or encourage us to consider aspects we hadn't thought about. Both books and the scholars who interpret them provide new frameworks for understanding human behavior.

Observing the thought processes of experts like these teaches us to approach information more discerningly and build analytical skills. This capacity to think deeply and critically is invaluable in a world constantly bombarded with information. A wise mentor or teacher often reminds us to question, explore, and embrace complexity.

You may be surprised to find that your perspective can be changed by an acquaintance you make in a group as informal as a book club. Marge Sosnik, for example, was one of the original members of our book club. She was a wonderful, thoughtful and intelligent person. She traveled with me several times, both to Europe and to New York. She had a local radio program where she interviewed writers, painters and performers. She also reviewed books. The episodes were always interesting. One can glean a great deal of insight from listening to artists speak about their inspiration and process. Sadly, she was one of the first of our members to pass away. My former student, Ben Folds, the incredibly gifted musician (about whom I will talk in more detail later), recently purchased her home.

Wisdom is not limited to factual knowledge but includes emotional intelligence, consideration, and interpersonal skills. Listening to or reading the words of someone who deeply understands human nature can teach us valuable soft skills, such as communication, compassion, and conflict resolution. A wise interviewer and reviewer like Marge Sosnik has learned to listen actively, motivate others, and navigate difficult conversations. Emotional awareness is incredibly important in building meaningful relationships.

Thoughtful leader-directed discussions in an organization such as a book club nurture emotional intelligence, primarily developed through experience and reflection. Much like the benefits of reading books, learning from someone who has mastered these skills helps us interact with others, better understand ourselves, manage our emotions, and build resilience. We become empowered, more compassionate and thoughtful.

A wise speaker or writer often inspires us to reach our potential, reminding us that growth is a lifelong journey, and everyone faces challenges. Their accomplishments show us what is possible. Their dedication, hard work, and integrity can spark motivation within us, encouraging us to pursue our goals with renewed energy.

A compelling speaker often instills a sense of curiosity and a commitment to lifelong learning. They encourage us to remain students of life, seeking wisdom wherever we can find it.

Clever people are usually intellectually curious, and their enthusiasm for learning can be contagious. They often emphasize the value of humility and openness and remind us that there is always more to learn and understand.

Among Phil Archer's many talents, for example, is his artistry in crafting miniatures. He has built intricately detailed follies of sweeping estates in England that a nobleman might have had made. They are complete with columns, domes and incredibly ornate gazebos all made from the finest mahogany or cherry, or other exotic wood. He's an amazing artist in his own right.

Being part of a book club offers many advantages beyond the simple pleasure of reading. It opens doors to increased knowledge, intellectual growth, and valuable social connections.

The experience of reading together, sharing insights, and learning from different perspectives makes book clubs a powerful tool for expanding one's horizons in ways that solitary reading simply cannot. Members read books they might not usually choose, exposing them to new genres, authors, and ideas. Whether history, philosophy, science fiction, or memoir, each book introduces fresh insights and perspectives. Members gain a deeper understanding of the book's themes, characters, and context as each participant contributes unique interpretations.

Such collaborative analysis can broaden one's understanding beyond what could be gleaned individually.

A discussion format challenges participants to articulate their thoughts and defend their interpretations, strengthening their analytical skills and often developing a more nuanced view of the material. As they regularly meet and discuss, they develop rapport and trust, which can lead to friendships and even professional opportunities.

We have had amazing people in our book club throughout the years (some of whom I have already mentioned) and have created new lasting friendships, as well as deepening old ones. One of our original members was Nancy Bragg. Her brother had been my first husband, Bob's roommate. Nancy eventually married Nick Bragg and moved to Winston-Salem. They always had a big party during the Christmas holidays, and I often attended with my former student and lifelong friend, lighting designer, Howell Binkley.

Nick first came to Winston-Salem as Director of Old Salem. Then he became Director of Reynolda House Museum of Art. He's a painter and there was a fabulous documentary about him in the RiverRun International Film Festival here in Winston-Salem. Incidentally, it is an incredible festival and one of the arts organizations I support.

The day I went to the screening of the documentary about Nick, I ended up sitting by none other than Phil Archer. We watched it together, which of course, enhanced an already wonderful experience.

Besides sharing the connection of both being respected local artists, they also shared an exhibit created by the Winston-Salem Foundation. It featured both Nick Bragg's paintings and Phil Archer's wooden models. It was an impressive exhibit.

Diane Jordan was another one of our original members. She taught drama at Salem Academy. My aforementioned student, Howell Binkley, who went on to become a Tony Award-winning lighting designer, would help out with the staging and lighting. Diane adored him.

Networking in a book club can be meaningful because it is based on shared interests and intellectual pursuits. Thoughtful discussions reveal values, opinions, and perspectives, leading to deep connections. The relationships formed can open doors to new career paths, recommendations, collaborations, and mentorships stemming from a genuine shared interest in reading and learning.

It's easy to let reading fall by the wayside in our busy lives. However, the structure of a book club—with set meetings and reading goals—provides accountability. Knowing that there's a discussion coming up motivates one to stay on track and complete their reading assignments. This structure can help turn reading into a consistent, enjoyable habit, a foundation for intellectual growth.

The social engagement of a book club, coupled with the intellectual stimulation of reading, can improve cognitive health and reduce feelings of isolation. Diversity of thought and experience makes discussions interesting and encourages members to see the world through a more inclusive lens.

In a world where technology often isolates people, book clubs provide a refreshing counterbalance. Though one person may prefer to read classical literature, others may enjoy lighter fare. I have found my book club so enjoyable and rewarding, that I recommend book clubs to everyone. Indeed, I have some suggestions for thinking about what type of book club may be a good fit for you.

How do you know if a particular club is right for you? Maximizing the enjoyment and benefits of participating is essential. Do you prefer small, intimate gatherings or more extensive, structured groups? Each offers distinct advantages.

Before committing, you should consider size, meeting structure, and focus. We've always limited our group to fourteen, which is large enough for interesting perspectives and small enough to allow everyone to engage.

For the best experience, clarify your own goals and preferences. What do you hope to gain from the experience? Are you looking to meet new people, or is your primary interest in intellectual growth and deep literary analysis? Some book clubs are heavily discussion-based and dive deep into literary elements, while others are more casual and social, focusing on enjoying books and spending time with friends. Consider whether you want a book club that reads a specific genre (like mystery or science fiction) or covers a variety of genres.

Here are some good questions to ask yourself:

Are you looking to read more consistently? Are you interested in challenging yourself with new genres? Do you want a more casual, friend-focused, professional, or discussion-oriented group? Would you prefer in-person gatherings or a virtual setup that may offer more flexibility?

Small book clubs, typically consisting of five to ten members, offer an intimate and relaxed setting ideal for in-depth conversations and personal connections. Members get to know each other well, becoming a supportive and close-knit community. Small clubs usually allow everyone ample time to share their thoughts, making discussions more personal and engaging. I have friends in my book club who, like me, have been there since the beginning. It's a wonderful bond that we share. I have other friends who have since dropped the book part of "book" club and now, thirty years later, just get together for wine! But it was the love of books that brought them together.

With fewer people, members can delve deeper into the book's themes and characters without feeling rushed. Small groups offer more chances to build genuine friendships. You see the same faces regularly, and conversations can be more open and supportive. They tend to find it easier for introverted or quieter members to participate, as there's less pressure to "compete" for speaking time. However, if a few members miss a meeting, the group dynamic can shift significantly, making discussions less lively. With fewer people, the range of viewpoints may be more limited, but small book clubs are an excellent fit for those who enjoy meaningful discussions in a comfortable setting and want to make close connections over time.

Large book clubs often consist of ten to twenty or more members. Though, as aforementioned, we have fourteen in ours, people are welcome to bring guests for special events, which make for a larger gathering. This larger format offers a more dynamic and structured environment. Larger clubs are sometimes affiliated with libraries or bookstores, giving them a more formal feel and access to more resources. They have organized agendas and sometimes even guest speakers or authors, similar to the events where Dr. Wilson and Phil Archer spoke.

With more members, each person may have less time to share their thoughts, which can lead to a more structured or surface-level discussion. While large groups offer many networking opportunities, it can take longer to build personal connections, as you may see different members at each meeting. The structured format and resources make these clubs a good fit for people who thrive in a more organized setting.

Another factor to consider is whether you want to join a book club focused on a particular genre or theme or a more general one exploring various genres. Specialized clubs, such as those focused on fantasy, historical fiction, or nonfiction, allow you to dive deeper into a genre you love and connect with others who share that interest. They're ideal for people with a specific reading passion and those who want to engage in complex discussions unique to that genre. General book clubs, on the other hand, encourage you to read outside your comfort zone and may introduce you to books you wouldn't have otherwise chosen. They're a great fit for readers who enjoy various genres and want to expand their reading habits.

Lastly, it's worth considering the format that best suits your lifestyle. In-person clubs offer face-to-face interaction, making it easier to build relationships. Still, they require members to meet in a specific location, which can be challenging for those with busy schedules. Virtual clubs offer flexibility and the opportunity to connect with people worldwide; they may, however, feel less personal.

A well-chosen book club can enrich your reading experience, introduce you to new ideas, and connect you with a community of fellow book lovers.

LESSON 8

INCLUSIVE COMMUNITY

We all should know that diversity makes for a rich tapestry, and we must understand that all the threads of the tapestry are equal in value no matter their color.

—Maya Angelou

I was teaching at the right time. In the late 1960s, I was in my thirties. We were teaching what was known as 2-2-2 for a while, and I loved it. For two years, some schools became just seventh and eighth grades, others ninth and tenth, and others eleventh and twelfth. It was so wonderful for discipline and academics. The athletic teams and the band had a hard time with it. But it was great for behavior, discipline, academics—and leadership. Because when you had ninth- and tenth-grade students, and there were no eleventh or twelfth graders to lead the school, these ninth and tenth graders would rise to leadership, which was beautiful.

I also taught when we consolidated the city schools with the county schools. My city school consolidated with two county schools to form a new one, which was a big move. We knew then that desegregation was in the future. With this knowledge, the YWCA started sponsoring dialogue groups. They would pair a white church and a black church and have a facilitator to moderate the discussion among people from the two churches.

During these dialogues, I was taking a year off from teaching. I received a call from the YMCA saying, "We would like you to be a facilitator for one of these groups."

I said, "Yes, I would love to if you would teach me how to do it."

They assured me they would work with me on the process and told me when to come to a meeting, which I did.

The two churches in my charge were Metropolitan United Baptist Church, an all-black congregation from East Winston, and Clemmons

Presbyterian Church, a suburban white church. It was a most fascinating experience! They had it planned so beautifully. Each of those churches sent about twelve people to the dialogue group. We had a couple of older adults, midlife adults, young adults, teenagers, and elementary school children. They had the whole population represented, and I was the facilitator. We met every other week. As they got to know one another, they would begin to ask questions.

After a few meetings, somebody in the group would say, "I've always wondered, how do you feel about [this or that]?"

They would ask each other questions about various things, and their discussions were always interesting, captivating, and beautiful.

We would alternate our meeting locations. One week, we'd go to Metropolitan, and the people from Clemmons would come to East Winston. Then, the next time, we'd all go out to Clemmons. We sat around a big table that was conducive to open discussion. It wasn't a hostile group. These people wanted to do this. As I facilitated the group and observed its evolution, I had the privilege of watching bridges built within our community: bridges of understanding, bridges of commonality, and most importantly, bridges of friendship and respect.

I didn't know I would return to teaching then, but in 1970, I was selected to become one of the first white English teachers to help with the desegregation of schools. I was to teach at Atkins, a high school traditionally known as a black school. They had hired several white faculty members in their first year to start the integration process. Before integrating the students, they wanted to give students and teachers a year to acclimate. Some white teachers went to black schools, and some black teachers went to white schools, so no one lost their jobs. We were just redistributed within the various schools, and it wasn't difficult for the faculty to accept me.

The woman who was supposed to come to Atkins to teach English was older and could not make that change so Palmer Friende, the associate superintendent of the Winston-Salem Forsyth County Schools, called me and asked me to do it. I felt honored that he would entrust me with this historical integration process.

Palmer and his wife, Bette, were dear friends of mine outside of our school lives. She taught at Whitaker Elementary School. They were fabulous people. Palmer was a handsome black man with bright blue eyes. He grew up in Kernersville, North Carolina. He said that when he was growing up, white people didn't want their children playing with this little colored boy, and the black families weren't sure they wanted their children playing with the colored boy with those weird blue eyes.

I attended many state conferences back then, including English conferences. If Palmer was there, we'd always have lunch at a restaurant in that town or city.

Palmer would always laugh and say, "Well, we turned a few heads today!"

I don't remember where we first met, but it was probably at a performance. We both loved the arts.

Having had a wonderful and enlightening experience facilitating the dialogue group for the YWCA, I had an idea.

I thought, "Ooh, I know how to meet my students' families. Go to their churches."

At that time the church was fundamental to the African American communities in the area. So, I went to a different church in East Winston every Sunday for several months. United Metropolitan Church, Shiloh, Mount Zion, First Baptist, Goler. Of course, I stood our like a sore thumb. I was the only Caucasian person there. I remember one church, Shiloh, where At that the minister asked me to stand. So, I did.

I said, "Thank you, thank you."

That's how I met parents, pastors, grannies, aunties, and uncles. I got to know them, and they got to know me. I wanted my students and their families to understand who I was. It's essential to *meet people where they are.* I had the utmost respect for my students, and I entered their world rather than asking people to enter a different world.

Then, on Monday morning, I loved going to school because some students would say, "You know who I saw?" or, "It was nice to see you at church yesterday."

And other students in the school I didn't teach would come by my room and wave because they'd met me at church.

My door was usually open, and sometimes, they would step inside just enough to tell the class, "She was at my church yesterday."

Word got around, and it made a difference.

If anybody indicated that they might even give me a hard time, all the people who knew from church would say, "No, no, no, she's alright."

It went on for so long that it became a joke. I told my students, "Sometimes, I think I ought to change my name to Miss Alright!"

The church visits served all of us well.

The second thing that had a significant impact on my first year at Atkins was the North Carolina School of the Arts, which was producing *Guys and Dolls* that year. Gary Beach had the lead. He became a Broadway actor and won a Tony Award for his work in *The Producers.* He has since passed away. The female lead was Berlinda Tolbert, who later played Jenny Willis Jefferson, the daughter of the biracial couple who lived upstairs on *The Jeffersons* television show. She was a beautiful young woman with a lovely singing voice. I taught twelfth-grade English, and more boys than girls were in my class. I took the entire class on an activity bus, including about half of the football team, to see the show. Well, a lot of the boys fell in love with Berlinda Tolbert. Of course they did! She had the face and voice of an angel! After that, I suddenly became a cool teacher!

They'd say, "When are we gonna go back to that school to see another one of those plays?!" It was incredible.

It was forward thinking of the School of the Arts to have Belinda in a traditionally white leading role. It was decades before shows like *Hamilton* reimagined how we look at casting. At the same time, I don't think the School of the Arts' casting process had anything to do with ethnicity; they simply cast the best among their students for each available role. They were color-blind at a time when many people weren't.

When I went to teach at Atkins, I started reading many black writers I had meant to read but hadn't gotten around to, like James Baldwin and Lorraine Hansberry. I felt it was imperative to introduce my students to people who shared their heritage, black writers, people to aspire to. I wanted them to feel like they could connect with both the writer and the material.

When I listen to the stories of people of color, they often say, "I was acting, but no one looked like me on TV."

Of course, that has changed a great deal. There are now many public role models in various walks of life with whom they can connect. I needed to read those writers to find another bridge to meet them. So, my reading was for the students *and* me.

Then, when the first white students came, I stayed at Atkins. I taught one year with all black students before the students integrated and three years with total integration. When we integrated, Atkins also joined the 2-2-2 system and had just ninth and tenth grade, so I became a ninth and tenth grade English teacher. It wasn't difficult for the students to integrate. In my experience,young people aren't like older people. I saw, firsthand, that it was simple for them to accept one another for who they were.

Half of the students in my classroom were black, and half were white. I used to tell them, "If you're white, you need to get busy finding a black friend. If you're black, get busy finding a white friend."

We would talk about racial, gender, and generational gaps.

I would say, "Every girl in this class needs to find a good friend and develop a good friendship with a guy because a good friend who's a guy can clue you in on many things about other guys and the male perspective in general. If you're a girl, work on a good friendship with a guy. Same thing, you guys; you need to work on a good friendship with a girl who can be honest with you. And racially, it's the same thing. If you're white, developing a good friendship with somebody in the school who's black is essential. By the same token, every student in this class needs to get to know some adult in this school, such as a teacher, coach, guidance counselor, or custodian. It might be a staff member in the cafeteria or a secretary in the office. But you just need to do that. That's the first homework assignment. You've got to start looking for ways to build across those gaps—racial gaps, gender gaps, generational gaps."

They sometimes sighed, rolled their eyes, and thought, "Oh boy, here she goes again." But it generally worked well.

We did not have problems at Atkins.

I think there were people in the school system who thought, "Oh, there'll be problems there."

There were problems at some of the schools, but we didn't have any significant ones. There were no fights or anything like that. Generally speaking, it went amazingly well.

One black student, Michael, would look out for me whenever we went to a play or concert. At that time, my car was a big Cadillac. I could pile eight or ten people into it and often did. (I would not recommend this today, but people weren't so concerned about seatbelts and carpool limits then.)

Michael lived in East Winston. He'd say, "Now, Miss Dunning, you pick me up first, and I'll be your navigator, Miss Dunning, there's just some streets over here that I wouldn't go on by myself at night. So, you need to pick me up first, and I'll direct you."

And he'd want me to let him out last. He'd get out and come around to my side of the car and say, "Now, be sure your door's locked and you drive carefully."

"Yes, Michael." He was such a caring person.

Those were wonderful, exciting years. I had so many fabulous students, many of whom became teachers, nurses, or businesspeople.

Denise Hartsfield was one of my black students. She went to university, then law school, and then she became a judge here.

Whenever I ran into her, she'd say, "My teacher!"

Talk about a powerful motivational speaker! She can take over any room or auditorium. She's amazing. She recently retired.

Davida Wagner also attended university and law school and became the county attorney for Forsyth County. She married Harold Martin, a young man who attended Carver High School. I didn't teach him.

Years ago, I ran into her, and she said, "Look! I'm engaged!"

She was so excited that I said, "Now, wait a minute, Davida. Are you sure that this young man is good enough for you? You are amazing!"

She enthusiastically replied, "Oh Mrs. Dunning, he is fabulous!"

He later became Dr. Martin, the chancellor of Winston-Salem State University. He served as chancellor for several years and then resigned to become the chancellor of North Carolina Agricultural and Technical State University in Greensboro. He has since retired, but I loved it when I met him while he was the chancellor here.

I told him (about my conversation with his young then-fiancée), "I didn't know you, and I wasn't sure!"

They are wonderful. Their two sons then went to Morehouse College in Atlanta, a prestigious school.

As you can see by these accomplished graduates, Atkins, like any other school, had brilliant students, some of whom had achievements that left you wondering about the road they took to get there. I remember having lively arguments in the teachers' lounge about where one girl would go to university and what she would major in.

Her science teacher enthusiastically said, "Of course, she will major in chemistry, biology, physics, or premed."

Her French teacher said, "Languages. Or English history."

At the end of the school year, we knew she was going to Duke—on a full scholarship. She was brilliant and so darling. When we found out she'd been accepted, five of us got together in the home of one of the teachers. I was the only white teacher in the group. We decided to pool our resources and get her luggage, darling pajamas, and a robe.

We said, "We just can't let that child go trotting off to Duke without."

She lived with her grandmother, who didn't have money, but we could at least make sure her granddaughter had lovely luggage, darling pajamas, a robe, and bedroom slippers! I can still picture her. She was charming, and she was good at absolutely everything.

One of the teachers in that group was a math teacher named Billie Matthews. I ended up teaching her two daughters at Reynolds. Beverly went on to medical school, and Donna went to veterinarian school. So, one became a people doctor, and one became an animal doctor. They were lovely girls, both excellent students and wonderful people.

Billie's husband, Clifton, was very protective of his girls.

I remember telling him, "Now, Clifton, we all know no boy will ever be good enough for your girls. I understand, but you'll have to ease up because those girls will want to date! And there are a lot of boys who are going to want to date them!"

I don't see Donna, the veterinarian, because she married and moved to Maryland. But I do see Beverly. She lives in Durham, North Carolina.

When her childhood girlfriends who live in Durham or Chapel Hill get together, they always call me, along with two of their elementary school teachers. We all gather for lunch all these years later. They are a delightful bunch.

After my last year at Atkins, I went to R. J. Reynolds to teach eleventh grade, and some of my Atkins students that I'd had in the tenth grade said, "Oh no!" because there I was again. So, I taught some of them twice, but I assured them, "You have valid reasons for requesting a schedule change!" It was so funny!

What have I learned from my experience with desegregation? Today, we call it diversity, equity, and inclusion. Lately, there has been much discussion and debate around this topic. The truth is the world has been diverse since humanity began. Each of us has a unique perspective.

Have you ever gone to see a movie, play, opera, or lecture and come out with a different vantage point on it than the person with whom you attended the event? We all process information differently. And isn't that wonderful?! What a spirited conversation you could have regarding your varying points of view.

Name almost any subject, and you can find opposing viewpoints and commonalities. It's woven into the fabric that makes up the United States and the entire human race. Society has struggled with divergent ways of thinking since the dawn of time. Wars have been fought; careers have been made or broken; friends and loved ones have grappled with complex discussions about essential subjects. But these discussions are critical, even as we struggle to find common ground where we meet. We share this world—all of us, every race, color, and creed, from all walks of life and all parts of the globe.

Diversity and inclusion are not new. They're not just fodder for academic seminars or buzzwords to be tossed around corporate boardrooms or tools to be used as political scare tactics.. They are ideals that represent powerful concepts that shape our society and give rise to progress, innovation, and prosperity. If we can open our minds to embrace our differences, we can experience the world through a new lens. Race, ethnicity, age, gender, sexual orientation, religion, socioeconomic status, and physical ability inform who a person is, how they think, and who they become. Each person brings distinctive skills, experience, perspective, and talent to a conversation. Embracing this myriad of perspectives paves the way for creativity, invention, and better judgment.

When individuals from multicultural backgrounds come together and share ideas, there is no limit to possibility. The results can be groundbreaking. For example, as many people know, in the late twentieth century, space agencies from the United States, Russia, Europe, Japan, and Canada joined forces toward a common goal: to create the International Space Station. Each country set aside its differences and brought together its brightest and best to collaborate on a highly ambitious scientific endeavor that would benefit all. Collectively, they advanced space exploration and scientific research in a previously unattainable way. Today, the space station is a testament to humanity's ability to unite and create something more significant than any one individual could do. It continues to serve as a platform for groundbreaking research in physics, biology, astronomy, and Earth observation, inspiring future generations of scientists and engineers around the globe.

Combining our minds and looking beyond our perspectives, we develop simple and complicated solutions that improve our world. Two heads are better than one, as the saying goes. Multiple innovative minds can move mountains. Working together allows people to consider a broader range of ideas and thoughts. If we never come together, how can we combat biases? We all have them, whether we want to admit it or not. Listening to another person's point of view can open our minds and help us make informed choices that reflect the needs of the many rather than the few.

Everyone deserves to have a sense of belonging and psychological safety. When individuals feel valued and respected for who they are, they are more likely to be engaged, motivated, and productive. It only takes a shift in one's mindset to actively and intentionally create an environment where everyone feels valued, respected, and empowered to contribute fully.

While diversity provides the foundation, inclusion is the catalyst that unlocks its full potential. Like those YWCA meetings I facilitated, promoting open communication, trust, and mutual respect can harness distinctly individual people's collective power to achieve common goals and objectives. Inclusive communities are more resilient and cohesive. They celebrate the richness of human individuality and promote social equity and justice. By breaking down barriers and bridging divides, inclusive societies create a sense of belonging and solidarity among all members, regardless of their background or identity.

Wouldn't you rather live in a culture of curiosity and openness than in one dominated by fear and anger? Everyone deserves the chance to thrive, regardless of who they are or where they come from. I feel blessed and enriched to have met people like my student, Michael, along my path. I never would have known him or had him volunteer to be my guardian angel had I not taken a chance and embraced the idea of integration. I am a better person for having taken that leap of faith.

LESSON 9

STEP OUTSIDE YOUR COMFORT ZONE

Life begins at the end of your comfort zone.
—Neale Donald Walsch, *Conversations with God*

We are all creatures of habit. Our familiar environments and routines give us a sense of safety and security. The unknown is a scary place for most. Lack of control of our surroundings often reveals our insecurities and makes us uncomfortable. Fear can handcuff a person and prevent them from accessing many enriching experiences.

Who knows what you might miss if you never step outside your comfort zone? The unknown can be a place of discovery and growth. Taking a risk and jumping off that imaginary cliff can be exhilarating and transformative. Though initially daunting, this uncharted territory can have surprising and refreshing benefits.

Beginning one's teaching career is undoubtedly daunting. Talk about a world of unknowns! No matter how much you are prepared, there are many hours of prep and a huge learning curve.

I began my teaching career at James A. Gray High School. I was there for a year and a half and liked it very much. Some excellent teachers took me under their respective and collective wings (great mentors!). Let me tell you, I couldn't have asked for a better beginning.

After a year and a half, I taught summer school at Reynolds High School. At that time, John Tandy was the assistant principal at Reynolds. Previously, he had been a massive football star at Chapel Hill, joining Charlie "Choo-Choo" Justice and his other teammates to make a football powerhouse.

The summer I taught at Reynolds, he said, "Miss Carswell, I'm going to be principal at Hanes High School this fall. I need you to come teach there."

I remember laughing. I said, "Oh, Mr. Tandy, I don't think you want me. I've only been teaching for a year and a half. I'm sure you'd rather have somebody with more experience than I have."

I don't remember what he said.

A week later, I received a letter from the Central Office saying, "You are being transferred to Hanes High School."

He was the best principal I ever had. He was fabulous. At Hanes, we all used to say that Mr. Tandy had the students in the palm of his hand. He had his faculty and the parents in the same place! And he juggled us all brilliantly. We worked hard and loved it because he was a fantastic administrator and leader. I learned a great deal from him.

I will never forget our first faculty meeting. He handed me my schedule, and I saw that I had five classes: tenth-grade English; eleventh-grade English; journalism(including publishing the school newspaper and the yearbook); and world history, which, as a history and English major, I loved.

There was also a general math class. I looked at that and said, "Oh my word! There must be some mistake!"

Mr. Tandy said, "Mrs. Carswell, that's not a joke. That is your schedule."

I said, "Mr. Tandy, that's five preparations. You didn't tell me that I'd have anything like this."

Teaching requires many hours of preparation per class. You must prepare your lesson plan before class, fulfilling the curriculum while managing your time appropriately. You need enough content in each class to stimulate the students' learning but not so much that you are rushing through the process. It's essential to make the pace of learning gradual so the students understand the concepts. If you jump too quickly from one concept to another, they will be unable to grasp what you are trying to teach them. If they miss early concepts, they can fall behind, as the process is cumulative. Conversely, if they move too slowly, you lose their interest and attention.

Sometimes, a teacher is assigned multiple classes on the same subject matter. This type of schedule allows a teacher the luxury of one prep for more than one class. However, a schedule where each class has different subject matter requires individual preparation per class: five different classes, five different preps.

Mr. Tandy said, "Of course I didn't tell you. You wouldn't have come if I'd told you!"

So there it was. I would be teaching five new classes, ready or not! I was intimidated, but I had committed to this job, so I rolled up my sleeves and decided to make the best of it. I admired and respected Mr. Tandy and was not about to disappoint him.

Ironically, in the end, general math class saved me. A math wizard I am not! But I can add, subtract, multiply, and divide. I can do percentages and fractions. That's general-level math. And the papers are easy to grade. 2 + 2 = 4. It has always equaled 4; it will always equal 4. The only answer is unequivocally 4. Not much reading is involved, and the answer is definitive. In marking-land, that's a huge advantage. Quick, quick, quick, quick.

Two English classes and a history class require essay papers. Journalism requires papers. Papers take a long time to mark, and the marking is more subjective. Unlike math, there is a gray area in marking where you, the teacher, must weigh, measure, and decide what is fair. Again, that takes time. Putting together a newspaper with a journalism class is rewarding and exciting but highly time-consuming. So I worked myself to the bone. There was a constant stream of papers, and I read them all the time. I took home stacks of homework every night. But the math? It was a piece of cake! I never would have predicted that I, of all people, would embrace math! It turned out to be my long suit. Had I insisted on another English class and not come out of my comfort zone to teach that subject, I'm sure I would have drowned in my marking!

Mr. Tandy was a wise man. He knew what he was doing when he assigned me those classes, and I'm glad I jumped into the deep end and learned how to swim. I became a better teacher because of it.

Confining ourselves to familiar practices or what we consider our expertise can inadvertently limit our exposure to new experiences, ideas, and people. My general-level math class had a different type of student than my English or journalism classes. My math students had a different way of tackling the learning process. It was satisfying to figure out how to teach them the math curriculum in a way that made sense to them.

By stepping out of our comfort zones, we open ourselves to new ways of thinking that challenge our preconceived notions and broaden our understanding. This exposure can nurture empathy, tolerance, and appreciation for the breadth of our human experience, enhancing our lives and interpersonal relationships.

When I taught twelfth-grade English, it was important to me to have my students memorize passages from various works of literature. There were poems and parts of poems that I wanted them to commit to memory. Memorizing great literature offers an array of benefits that develop one's intellectual and emotional landscape. It hones linguistic skills, increases vocabulary, and fosters a deeper language understanding. Immersing one's mind in the varied experiences and perspectives depicted within these timeless works cultivates emotional intelligence. Memorizing literature also improves cognitive function and memory retention. Analyzing complex themes, characters, and narratives encourages critical thinking.

And very importantly, the ability to recite passages or entire works from memory provides a source of personal fulfillment. I wanted my students to carry these passages in their minds so they could be anywhere, anytime, perhaps driving somewhere, and something would strike their eye or their ear, and they would recall the poem. It might help them draw inspiration and wisdom at any time. Ultimately, the practice of memorizing great literature transcends rote learning. It offers a transformative journey through human thought and emotion.

Sometimes, we would choose passages from American poetry, sometimes from English. My students memorized passages like:

> Two roads diverged in a yellow wood,
> And sorry I could not travel both
> And be one traveler, long I stood . . .
> —"The Road Not Taken," by Robert Frost

Even in the era when I was teaching, we all led busy lives that might prevent us from grabbing a book from home,the library, or a bookshop, and searching while thinking, "What was that quote?"

You could Google it today but, in this fast-paced environment, most people might not even bother doing that. Plus, it might have less impact if you just glance at it online. Things you commit to memory invoke a visceral response that connects you to the material. A memorized passage is always there for you to revisit at any moment. And knowing the right passage can make you feel like the cleverest person in the room if you recite it at the perfect moment.

So, I encouraged or required my students to memorize poetry passages from great writers. They usually had choices:

"Choose one or more Shakespearian sonnets you want to memorize."

But it wasn't always Shakespeare. It could have been Elizabeth Barrett Browning: "How do I love thee? Let me count the ways. . ."

Or John Keats.

Ben Folds, a now-famous former student whom I mentioned earlier, set a Keats passage to music for the class and stood before them quoting that sonnet:

When I have fears that I may cease to be
Before my pen has gleaned my teeming brain . . .

Keats is saying: I might not live to write all the things I want to write or to say all of the things I want to say. That poem inspired Ben to set it to music. He is now an accomplished musician and an author, having now written a book about his life.

When I taught British literature, we read some *Beowulf* and other Anglo-Saxon literature. *Beowulf* is in Old English, which can be very difficult for contemporary English speakers to comprehend and is not (in my opinion) as beautiful as Middle English, which evolved a few hundred years later. Because of this, I never had students memorize any of *Beowulf,* but when we talked about how language evolved by the time Chaucer was writing, I said, "I want you to memorize the first eighteen lines of the prologue to *The Canterbury Tales* by Geoffrey

Chaucer, and it goes like this:"

When April with his showers sweet with fruit
The drought of March has pierced unto the root
And bathed each vein with liquor that has power
To generate therein and sire the flower;
When Zephyr also has, with his sweet breath,
Quickened again, in every holt and heath,
The tender shoots and buds, and the young sun
Into the Ram one half his course has run,
And many little birds make melody
That sleep through all the night with open eye
(So Nature pricks them on to ramp and rage)—
Then do folk long to go on pilgrimage,
And palmers to go seeking out strange strands,
To distant shrines well known in sundry lands.
And specially from every shire's end
Of England they to Canterbury wend,
The holy blessed martyr there to seek
Who helped them when they lay so ill and weak.

We read it in today's English, but I also had copies in Middle English, the way it was originally written. And I had a recording of it, but before I played that recording for the students, I would read it aloud. "We are going to listen to it, but it goes something like this:"

Whan that Aprille with his shoures soote,
The droghte of March hath perced to the roote,
And bathed every veyne in swich licóur
Of which vertú engendred is the flour;
Whan Zephirus eek with his swete breeth
Inspired hath in every holt and heeth
The tendre croppes, and the yonge sonne
Hath in the Ram his halfe cours y-ronne,
And smale foweles maken melodye,

That slepen al the nyght with open ye,
So priketh hem Natúre in hir corages,
Thanne longen folk to goon on pilgrimages,
And palmeres for to seken straunge strondes,
To ferne halwes, kowthe in sondry londes;
And specially, from every shires ende
Of Engelond, to Caunterbury they wende,
The hooly blisful martir for to seke,
That hem hath holpen whan that they were seeke.

And when I finished quoting it, I said, "That's what I want you to memorize."

Of course, they'd always say, "There's no way!" or, "I can't do that. Sorry. I can't do that."

I said, "Oh, you *can* do that. You *must* can!"

And so they all did it.

"Eighteen lines," I said. "Then, if you are willing to go ahead and do forty lines and twenty-two more, there can be extra credit. But everybody is going to do the first eighteen. And I promise you, once you do that, it will etch itself on your brain and be with you forever."

I cannot tell you how many times I've had it quoted to me through the years. I've been in grocery stores, I've been in theaters, I've been at New Year's Eve dances. I remember being at a black-tie New Year's Eve party when two people who had been my students came up behind me, one in each ear, and together they started:

Whan that Aprille with his shoures soote,
The droghte of March hath perced to the roote . . .

And it was both surprising and incredibly gratifying! And this would not have happened if I hadn't pushed my students outside of their comfort zones!

Many years after I retired, I was honored at Reynolds High School and inducted into its Arts Hall of Fame. Although I feel like I don't belong there, they stopped listening to me a long time ago.

In fact, they told me: "Sorry, we don't listen to you anymore. *Now,* you do what *we* tell you to do, and *we* are doing *this*!"

Prior inductees included some of the former students I've mentioned: Howell Binkley, Michael Wilson, Lindsey Jones, Ben Folds, Lennie Foy, and several more of my former students. I think they deserve such an honor as painters, musicians, composers, designers, directors, and writers. I don't do any of that. I elevate minds. But, again, in my opinion, that's not what the award should be for. It was created to honor true, deserving, accomplished artists! However, as I stated earlier, they no longer listen to me! I did my best to inspire my students, some of whom became great artists, and their success is all the honor I require.

The night I was presented with the award had been preceded by some degree of publicity. Eight or nine of us were inducted that evening: musicians and actors . . . and Phyllis Dunning. A large audience was present, including some of my former students. I was sitting in the audience for most of the event, and at one point, they took me backstage. Each inductee was preceded by an introduction. For example, a musician would tell the audience about their music, all the famous bands they'd played with, concerts they'd done, and all of their accolades. Everyone in the audience applauded for each one. I was the last inductee to be presented.

When they announced my name, a group of people in the audience, all former students, stood up and started clapping and shouting. Then, in unison, they started reciting the Middle English prologue to *The Canterbury Tales* that I had had them memorize:

Whan that Aprille with his shoures soote,
The droghte of March hath perced to the roote . . .

Of course, the rest of the audience just cracked up! What a moment for the history books that was!

The beauty of Middle English is that a contemporary reader can read and understand it with relative ease, unlike Anglo-Saxon. Of course, when I taught it, we decoded it together in class. It's beautiful, meaningful poetry. And besides wanting my students to carry art in their heads forever, I also wanted them to do something they swore they could not do, to give them that sense of achievement. Birds push their offspring out of the nest when they are ready to learn how to fly. Instinct takes over, and the young ones learn the exhilaration of soaring through the sky. I gave my students a healthy nudge because I knew their capabilities when they were unaware of them. Had they not tried, how would they have learned to fly independently?

I wanted them to know, "Yes, you can do that, and you will."

So many people have hidden talents that simply need to be unearthed. It is truly remarkable to witness them as they test their wings.

I will never forget that Dawn Tomlinson was the first student I taught who, when it was her turn to recite, got up in front of the class, looked at us, and took command of the room by starting a beat. I sat with the class, and we all kept the beat. She looked right at us and performed it like a rap. It was, as far as I know, before the word *rap* was even common in English. And here we all were, keeping the beat.

Dawn was wonderful. Unfortunately, she passed away several years ago, but some years later, I ran into her husband, Steve Beck, at the grocery store. I had also taught Steve.

When I got to the cashier, Steve came along and said to the cashier, "That's with me."

I protested, "Steve!" I had forty or fifty dollars-worth of food in my basket. I'd already seen him in the grocery store, and we'd hugged and talked.

I said, "Steve Beck, you cannot do that."

And he said, "Of course, I can do that. I've already done that. I have often thought I would like to do something for Mrs. Dunning, but I haven't done anything. And I remember the note you wrote me when Dawn died, and I've thought about it, but I haven't done a thing, so at least I'm doing this, and I can check it off my to-do list." It was humbling.

As long as I live, I will never forget Dawn Tomlinson performing Middle English as a rap!

Occasionally, I would have a student for whom it was torture to stand before the class to say anything. Anything. Not very often, but occasionally. In those cases, I would arrange for that student to come after school, after class, or early in the morning to recite their lines. It was more important for those students to have a similar experience of accomplishment and a piece of literature to carry with them throughout their lives than it was for them to conquer a fear of public speaking at that moment. Perhaps that was too much "overcoming" to take on all at once.

But almost everybody did it in front of the class, which helped them with poise, grace, and carriage.

In fact, on any given day, somebody would say, "I want to do my lines today, but if some other people want to do it, I'd like to be third or fourth or fifth to do my lines and psych myself up and hear how other people do it."

Sometimes, it takes baby steps to move beyond our "safe place." Whether they're giant steps or small, venturing beyond our comfort zones is essential for personal growth and self-development. I encourage you to face your challenges by embracing discomfort, for that is where we discover our true strengths, capabilities, and potential. Whether learning a new skill, pursuing a passion, or taking on a new role or responsibility, pushing our limits helps us confront our fears and overcome obstacles in our growth. That's when we cultivate resilience, confidence, and a sense of empowerment that propels us toward achieving our goals and aspirations.

If you feel overwhelmed, it's okay to take a breath and return to the baby steps, but I encourage you to keep moving forward and exploring your potential. That's when you'll discover creativity and innovation.

Comfort breeds complacency, whereas discomfort (in healthy measures) fuels curiosity and experimentation. Pushing the envelope of familiar boundaries teaches us to adapt, problem-solve, and think creatively as we navigate unfamiliar terrain. This process of exploration and discovery stimulates our minds, igniting our creativity and spirit of innovation. And that, my friends, drives progress and success in our personal and professional lives.

One of the most surprising rewards of embracing the unknown is the sense of liberation and empowerment that comes from conquering our fears and pushing our boundaries. Public speaking, traveling alone to a foreign country, pursuing a passion despite the fear of failure—whatever we choose to do, the realization that we can overcome obstacles that once seemed insurmountable fills us with a sense of pride, confidence, and newfound freedom. It encourages us to continue pushing our limits and embracing new challenges.

Life is unpredictable, and change is inevitable. We cultivate resilience and adaptability by willingly exposing ourselves to a manageable level of discomfort and uncertainty. Navigating life's twists and turns with grace and grit becomes easier then. Why be paralyzed by fear or resistance to change? We learn to embrace uncertainty as an opportunity for growth and transformation, trusting in our ability to adapt, evolve, and thrive under any circumstance. We genuinely discover life's richness and beauty when we step outside ourselves. We unlock opportunities for personal growth, self-discovery, and fulfillment by embracing challenges and pushing our boundaries. The benefits and surprises that await us on the other side of our comfort zones are vast and profound, enriching our lives in ways we could never have imagined.

So, let us dare to venture forth, explore the unknown, and embrace the journey of self-discovery and transformation beyond our comfort zones.

LESSON 10

COUNT YOUR BLESSINGS

I am grateful for what I am & have. My thanksgiving is perpetual. It is surprising how contented one can be with nothing definite—only a sense of existence.

—Henry David Thoreau

My mother died at age 83 in 1994, and her last words to me were, "I count my blessings."

She counted her blessings from this life to the next, but it's also an instruction, isn't it? As I mentioned in the chapter of this book about my parents, my mother gave me the most significant tools for life by teaching me the power of positive thinking and living in gratitude. It is so ingrained into the fabric of my being that I rarely feel depressed or wanting.

Counting one's blessings and embracing positive thinking emerge as beacons of hope and resilience when we most need them. A gratitude practice is a pathway to happiness and well-being that can't be quantified. Acknowledging and appreciating the positive aspects of one's life, no matter how small or insignificant, is a powerful antidote to the human tendency to focus on shortcomings and inadequacies.

It's not always easy to stop and smell the roses in this often overwhelming, fast-paced life. But that's precisely when and why we need to do it. One must be mindful and disciplined in a world often consumed by negativity, stress, and constant striving. Yes, it takes discipline to rewire your thinking, but I promise you, the results will be well worth the effort.

Though sometimes it may feel like the world is caving-in around us, there are always things for which we can count our blessings. The simple fact of waking up in the morning is, in my opinion, a gift—not a right, not a guarantee—but a precious and beautiful *gift.* Even under the most difficult life-circumstances, you will discover that some people manage to live with a simple but powerful gratitude.

The rewards of living in gratitude can be astonishing. Research in positive psychology demonstrates that people who consciously feel gratitude experience greater happiness, satisfaction, and overall well-being than those who do not. Counting your blessings can promote a shift in perspective, enabling you to recognize potential amidst scarcity, or opportunity amidst crisis. By directing your attention to what is "going right" rather than dwelling on what is "going wrong," you can cultivate a mindset of abundance and possibility.

Take a slow, deep breath and absorb those concepts: abundance and possibility.

Doesn't that sound (and feel!) better than anxiety and fear? This shift in mindset enhances emotional resilience and fuels motivation and perseverance in the face of challenges.

Take another slow, deep breath. Try to think of all of the things that exist in this very moment for which you can be grateful. This can be as simple as a pleasing texture or smell, or as profound as a treasured memory of a loved one.

Gratitude inspires positive thinking and engenders a sense of control and agency over one's life. Most of the people I know who are of my generation (and who are still living productive lives) will tell you that they live in gratitude. Like me, a dear friend of mine starts her day with a gratitude prayer: counting her blessings for everything ranging from her grandchildren to the sunshine streaming-in through her window. This same friend also has a rule about lunching with other friends: no one at lunch is allowed to talk about "their latest procedure."

As she always says, "At our age, we all have something!"

She lives her life intentionally, despite the inherent difficulties of aging, by creating an atmosphere of positivity that follows her throughout her day.

By living in gratitude, people cultivate a profound appreciation for the journey rather than fixating solely on the destination. True success transcends material wealth or external achievements; it encompasses a deep sense of fulfillment and purpose.

Elizabeth Gilbert, author of the bestselling memoir *Eat, Pray, Love,* is known for her candid storytelling and infectious optimism. Personal struggles and setbacks, including a difficult divorce and creative challenges, marked Gilbert's journey. However, she remained resilient and committed to her writing, achieving widespread acclaim and success. She frequently speaks about the importance of gratitude and self-compassion in her work, encouraging readers to embrace authenticity and pursue their passions. Through her writing and speaking engagements, she inspires others to cultivate positivity, gratitude, and resilience in their own lives.

Many of us also share a unique and almost-universal blessing that we frequently forget: the functioning of our bodies. Our hearts beat a hundred thousand times daily without conscious effort; our ribs and sternum protect our hearts (doing a fabulous job 24/7); each of the miraculous cells in our bodies is constantly evolving. Cells are brilliant and efficient, carrying out specialized functions, housing our bodies' hereditary material, and making copies of themselves when needed. They provide structure, taking nutrients from food and converting them into energy. Cells are miraculous and resilient, and we all have them. Even if our bodies are not functioning optimally, we can all find reasons to be grateful for what our unique bodies allow us to do.

So, what do *you* have to be grateful for? Some people have difficulty thinking of anything when "put on the spot," but you only need to look around and look within. There are unlimited blessings in every life. How long has it been, for example, since you set aside time to appreciate the beauty of a sunrise or sunset? These are lovely magical moments that occur daily, no matter where you are, and they are 100 percent free. They are the perfect symbols of the steadfast promise of each new day and the peaceful closure of another.

If you are still unsure of where you should begin in your gratitude practice, I have listed some of my favorite blessings below. I have made them as universal as possible, and you are welcome to adopt and adapt any or all of them for your own use (if you find them helpful):

Life: The precious gift of my existence and existence itself: people, plants, animals

Health: The well-being of our bodies and minds
Family: The love and support of those closest to us
Friends: The companionship and connections that enrich our lives
Love: The profound bond that unites us with others
Nature: The beauty and wonder of the natural world
Home: A place of comfort, safety, and belonging
Food: Nourishment for our bodies and souls
Water: The essential source of life and vitality
Education: The opportunity to learn, grow, and expand our horizons
Creativity: The power to express ourselves through art, music, and innovation
Work: The ability to contribute our talents and skills to the world
Freedom: The privilege to live in a society where we can pursue our dreams and aspirations
Opportunity: The countless occasions to explore new possibilities and embrace new experiences
Memories: The moments of joy, laughter, and love that shape our lives
Kindness: The generosity and compassion of others that uplift and inspire us
Forgiveness: The grace to let go of resentment and embrace healing and reconciliation
Technology: The tools and advancements that enhance our lives and connect us with others
Music: The universal language that touches our hearts and soothes our souls
Books: The wisdom, knowledge, and escape found within their pages (or virtual pages!)
Laughter: The medicine that lightens our spirits and brings joy to our days
Challenges: The obstacles that strengthen our resilience and fuel our growth

Hope: The belief in better days ahead and the resilience to persevere through adversity

Gratitude: Acknowledging and appreciating the abundance surrounding us, filling our hearts with joy and contentment

Yes, I give thanks for *gratitude* itself. It makes an enormous difference in my life and the life of anyone who practices it. *Gratitude* is the doorway to miraculous living. A simple expression of thankfulness holds profound transformative power in our emotional well-being, brain structure, and function. You just need to step through the threshold each day and see your world in a different light. Trust me, *it feels so good!*

Given my age, you might be surprised to find *technology* on my list. Though I didn't grow up with much technology beyond an alarm clock and a record player, I have been blessed to have had the longevity to observe and benefit from the evolution of technology. I've seen firsthand how it has enhanced our lives. Some aspects of technology are debated as double-edged swords, but look at the incredible strides technology has facilitated! In the world of science and life-saving health care, technology has been a game-changer.

One of the greatest minds of our time, Stephen Hawking, theoretical physicist, cosmologist, and author, famously had ALS, Lou Gehrig's disease. Had it not been for modern technology, he would not have been able to communicate his groundbreaking scientific knowledge with the world.

The arts have also benefited tremendously from the dawn of digital media, whether the specific medium is music, filmmaking, scriptwriting, graphic arts, or multimedia. Even theater has seen technological advancements that enhance the live experience.

And though social media has its drawbacks, I am incredibly grateful for the ability to connect with so many wonderful loved-ones daily! In my later years (as I mentioned earlier), I've found myself with a paralyzed vocal cord. Though it is difficult to "croak" through a phone call, I can post my thoughts and communicate with people worldwide on social media.

Recently, after a beautiful event at one of the schools where I formerly taught, I posted: "I am grateful for another inspiring week of great music and theater and the added joy of seeing so many outstanding former students at their 40th RJR reunion! 'My heart leaps up ...'

I enjoy sharing my gratitude. It can be infectious, and there is not enough of it worldwide. Of course, one should be mindful when posting on a public forum. Words can lift one and make one's heart sing, but conversely, they can bite with the ferocity of a vicious animal. Be thoughtful about your posts. They can have a powerful impact, for better or worse.

In the wise words of English author and member of Parliament Edward Bulwer-Lytton, "The pen is mightier than the sword."

The "pen" might be virtual these days, but it has even more impact as it reaches a broader audience.

As you can see, *challenges* are also on my gratitude list. One cannot go through life's beautiful journey without climbing metaphorical mountains and navigating their peaks and valleys. How we choose to face our challenges is up to us. We are in the driver's seat of our own lives. Challenges inform our journey and help mold the people we become. Overcoming adversity can give us strength, purpose, compassion, and understanding. When we emerge from our challenges, we do so as different, hopefully enriched, people.

I often find authors inspiring, so (as you can see) I have chosen a quote at the top of each chapter of this book. Paraphrasing the sentiment of Ralph Waldo Emerson: Cultivate the habit of being grateful for every good thing that comes to you and give thanks continuously. And because all things have contributed to your advancement, you should include all things in your gratitude.

Yes, *all* things have contributed to your advancement, including challenges and adversity. Sometimes, the challenges in our lives propel us forward faster than the harmony. We learn from them, grow, and become stronger, wiser individuals. Though they often feel uncomfortable, there is much to be said about life's challenges.

Hope is also on my list. For those feeling overwhelmed or misunderstood, I just want to assure you that there *will* be better days ahead.

Phyllis' parents celebrating their 50th wedding anniversary

Phyllis' official school portrait

The Dunnings

The Dunnings; Anne and Larry Walker; Glory and Larry Singer

Above and right: Phyllis at home

Left to right: Phyllis on a cruise in Greece , Phyllis preparing to board a cruise

Phyllis and her book club

Phyllis between Frank Bennedetti and Gary Trowbridge

Zoe King, Howell Binkley, Joyce Storey, and Phyllis

Phyllis and Joyce Storey

Phyllis, Howell Binkley, and Zoe King standing in front of the marquee for Hamilton

Phyllis and David Parsons

Phyllis with Howell Binkley holding one of his Tony Awards for Best Lighting Design

Phyllis and Ben Folds

Phyllis and Michael Wilson

If you hold onto that ideal and believe it, you will find strength that will help you navigate whatever challenges you face. And if your burden feels too heavy, don't hesitate to ask for help. We can sometimes feel like an island, or that we are carrying the weight of the world on our shoulders alone, but there is always help. I encourage you to share your burden with a friend, family member, or professional. We are all on this journey together and everyone needs a helping hand at one point or another.

One of your most potent weapons is your *mindset.* Is your glass half empty or half full? You get to choose, you know. It often appears when you look for the silver lining in any given situation.

I would be remiss if I didn't say a few (actually *quite* a few!) words about the power of *laughter.* A good laugh is good for the soul. One fun-filled exercise (sometimes used at summer camp) has everyone seated in a circle: The first person says, "Ha!"

The second person says, "Ha! Ha!"

The third person says, "Ha! Ha! Ha!" and the laughter increases as they go around the circle. Typically, everyone begins laughing, enjoying every ridiculous second!

Internationally published science writer David DiSalvo explains the phenomenon of this type of game from a scientific vantage point: "It's like a game of endorphin dominoes. That's why when someone starts laughing, others will laugh even if they're not sure what everyone is laughing about."

Endorphins are natural "feel-good chemicals" released into the brain when we laugh. They are natural mood boosters.

Indeed, the adage "laughter is the best medicine" is believed to have originated in the Bible:

> A cheerful heart is good medicine, but a crushed spirit dries up the bones.
> —Proverbs 17:22 (New International Version)

This expression is more than just a cliché. Laughter's superpower has sustained credibility with spiritual leaders and medical professionals alike for centuries. Historians suspect that our predecessors even laughed well before they could speak. They shared their joy, forged friendships, and conveyed a sense of safety and well-being all through laughter.

In the 1300s, the French surgeon Henri de Mondeville recommended telling jokes to patients after a procedure. More recently, Dr. Hunter "Patch" Adams, a physician and comedian, used humor and laughter as a central part of his patient care. His story was popularized in the film *Patch Adams,* starring Robin Williams. Even the father of psychoanalysis, Sigmund Freud, was a proponent of laughter to reduce stress in times of crisis.

Today, many people join laughter yoga clubs, engaging in intentional laughter exercises or activities that create joy, reduce stress, and improve overall well-being. Dr. Madan Kataria from Mumbai, India, began this movement by maintaining that voluntary laughter can be just as beneficial as spontaneous laughter, enhancing mental and physical health. People who have tried it have improved mood, reduced anxiety, strengthened immunity, and significantly increased social connection. A playful, inclusive environment nurtures people to lower their inhibitions and welcome the therapeutic power of laughter. It relaxes the body and creates a sense of community and support.

Of course, you don't need to join a laughter group to find the humor in things. Through the years, for example, I've had numerous students who could humorously imitate me. One student, Victor, was the only one I remember who was a black male with the impersonation down pat!

Anytime students wanted to do skits about faculty, whoever was imitating me would pull all their hair to one side of their head (I have always worn it in what we called a "set" in my time—it was and continues to be short, curled, and swept to one side, with much hairspray involved!). Another student, Howell Binkley, used to call my hair "the helmet" and me "Helmet Head" because my hair never moved! Part of the students' skits was always, "She does have two ears. There's one under there!"

There were two physical gags my students would do to imitate me:

one (of course) was my hair, and the other was lots and lots of scarves! I always wore a dress, three-inch heels, and (each day) a scarf. The skits were always brilliant!

Our administration once asked faculty to bring baby pictures, which they displayed in the main hall in a big case with numbers. Students could go by, write down the numbers, and guess which faculty member was in each picture.

One of my black students, a boy, came by, and he said, "I know. I know which one of those pictures is you."

I said, "You do not!"

He said, "I know you are number 12 because this little white girl is sitting there. She got a little gold necklace and a little gold bracelet. I know that's you because I bet you were born with that gold stuff on!"

I dressed up every day, which was evident to him. It was, in fact, my picture, but it was so funny that he could guess just from one glance. He could not wait to tell me!

My students made me laugh a lot, and the more you look, the more you will discover that there is humor all around you. Young people, especially, enjoy laughter. That is one of the things I love about teaching. My students were terrific people to be around, and their lightheartedness was infectious.

When was the last time you had a good laugh that you could feel from your head to the tips of your toes? It might do you a world of good. The mind-body connection is undeniable. Positive thinking is not just a state of mind; it's a way of life. It's about focusing on the bright side of situations, choosing optimism, and believing in one's ability to overcome challenges. When a person consciously elects to interpret events in a positive light, they experience lower levels of distress and higher levels of life satisfaction.

Gratitude also has the potential to transform both personal and professional endeavors. It creates a remarkable cycle of abundance consciousness, where success precipitates more success. By acknowledging and celebrating their achievements, successful people attract more blessings. This abundance mindset not only expands their realm of influence, but it also inspires others to emulate their example.

Here are some practical gratitude strategies that you might find helpful for counting your blessings:

Keep a Gratitude Journal: This is one of the most effective ways to cultivate gratitude. Take a few moments each day to reflect on the blessings you've experienced, both large and small. Choose three things you are thankful for and write them down, along with a brief explanation of why you are grateful for them. Through this simple practice, you cultivate gratitude and accumulate powerful reminders of the abundance in your life.

You might write something like, "Today, I am grateful for the warmth of the morning sun, the laughter of my loved ones, and the smell of freshly brewed coffee. (I'm a huge fan of the last one!) These simple pleasures remind me of the beauty and richness of life, filling my heart with gratitude and joy."

Practice Mindful Awareness: When mindful, you stay in the moment, paying attention with openness, curiosity, and acceptance. If you cultivate mindful awareness, you become more connected to the beauty and blessings that surround you daily. There are many simple pleasures in life that you can savor: a blooming flower, a gentle breeze, or a sincere conversation with a friend.

In your journal, you can write something like, "As I walk through the park, I pause to admire the vibrant colors of the spring blossoms and the delicious fragrance of wildflowers. In the stillness and presence of this moment, I am filled with gratitude for the wonders of the natural world and the gift of being alive."

Express Gratitude to Others: I practice this a lot and am very sincere in my appreciation. Take time to acknowledge and thank people who have positively impacted you. We are often grateful for these people but somehow neglect to tell them: friends, family members, coworkers, strangers. The most straightforward word of thanks can make a person's day soar and deepen your bond with them. I'm a big proponent of thank-you notes. I always have a box of cards close by. Take that moment to write a heartfelt thank you note. It is so fulfilling to write a note like that, to let the person know how much impact they've had on your life experience. And let me tell you, receiving a note like that in the mail can lift a person's spirits quicker than anything. (Emails, texts, and phone calls also count!) You will reap the rewards of your gratitude with a sense of warmth and connection.

Find Beauty in Adversity: This may take time, but it will be well worth your efforts. Even amid difficulties and challenges, you can find life's blessings. Practice reframing an adverse situation. See it as a learning moment, an opportunity for growth and resilience. Though embracing our lessons is often tricky, silver linings can and do emerge from life's trials. Know that they are ultimately contributing to your personal growth and development.

In your journal, you could write, "Despite the setbacks I'm facing in my career, I am thankful for the opportunity to learn and grow from these experiences. The obstacles I encounter serve as stepping stones toward my success. They help me strengthen my resolve and become a better professional and a wiser person."

The law of attraction suggests that positive thoughts attract positive outcomes. When people radiate positivity, they uplift their spirits and attract opportunities and favorable circumstances. Optimistic people exude confidence, making them more appealing to others personally and professionally. Their positive energy draws others toward them, opening doors to new relationships, career advancements, and other avenues of success.

Gratitude leads to optimism and positive thinking, nurturing a sense of empowerment and self-efficacy. Believing in yourself is a cornerstone for success. Maintaining a positive mindset makes you more likely to set ambitious goals and pursue them with excitement. Belief in your abilities fuels your motivation, leading to more extraordinary accomplishments and personal fulfillment. Success begins with unwavering confidence in your potential.

Counting blessings is a profound and life-changing way to enrich your life. It permeates every aspect of our experience, from mental and emotional well-being to physical health and professional success. By acknowledging and appreciating the richness around us, we open our hearts to joy, contentment, and a sense of inner peace.

As we navigate the complexities of our collective existence, the profound words of Norman Vincent Peale come to mind:

"Change your thoughts and you can change the world."

LESSON 11

SELF CARE WHILE FACING CHALLENGES

Life isn't about waiting for the storm to pass . . .
It's about learning to dance in the rain.
—Vivian Greene

The '60s was a significant decade for me: a new school, a divorce, Europe, and a new husband. Lots happened in that decade.

I was married to my first husband, Bob Carswell, for eleven years. Nice guy. That was his problem. Everybody loooooved Bob Carswell. He was sweet, tall, dark, and handsome. And he was a guy who couldn't say no. I was the first of five wives spread out over his six marriages. His three brothers and his sister remained my friends after my divorce from Bob. His mother, too, was my dear, dear friend: Mother Carswell and I probably had lunch at least once a week. It didn't bother Bob. I had a much better relationship with his family than he did.

His mother always used to say, "Phyllis, I've told them all multiple times, you are forever and ever my daughter."

After wife number five, Bob remarried wife number three, with whom he had a son. Both Bob and his wife have since passed away.

Mother Carswell and Dad Carswell were separated for over twenty years and finally divorced. He needed to be more committed and responsible.

She said of her four sons, " My fervent prayer was always: 'Don't let any of the boys follow in their father's footsteps.'" But she said to me, "Oh, Phyllis, the one who *did* would, of course, be the one you married!"

Bob followed in his father's footsteps when it came to commitment and responsibility! Even so, several of my best friends said, "Of all the couples we know, you two were the last we ever thought would split up."

However, we did split up, and I found myself at a crossroads in my life. Having experienced a major life upheaval, I felt adrift after Bob and I divorced. My first instinct was to take a year off.

I thought, "Oh, I would love to get out of town." But then I told myself, "No, I can't do that. That would be running away, and one does NOT run away."

Life is replete with challenges, from personal struggles to professional hurdles. How we confront these obstacles significantly shapes our growth and resilience. Choosing to face life's bumps in the road rather than running away demonstrates courage. It is a critical pathway to personal development and fulfillment. So, I decided to stay and keep teaching for another two years.

Life's obstacles are an inherent part of the human experience. Relationship problems are only one aspect of what could be negatively affecting your journey. Maybe you are dealing with health issues, financial difficulties, or a career setback. While our instinct to avoid pain and discomfort is natural, consistently running away can lead to a cycle of avoidance and missed growth opportunities. Avoidance might provide you with temporary relief, but it often results in increased stress and anxiety as unresolved issues continue to linger. Every challenge presents an opportunity to learn and evolve.

In my own life, I faced my new single world with mindful determination. I benefited from that time of introspection and reflection while I dove into my teaching, which was always a joy. I adjusted to my new circumstances and gradually gained strength and perspective.

It is essential to allow yourself time to grieve. A loss is a loss, whether it's the loss of a relationship and the dreams that came with it or the death of a loved one. It's normal to feel a range of emotions, from sadness and anger to relief and confusion, but you must allow yourself to experience these feelings without judgment. Healing doesn't happen overnight. Take the necessary time to process your loss. Only you know how much time you need. You can't rush the process, no matter how much you might like to.

If you find it particularly hard to cope, you might consider seeking the help of a therapist, counselor, or religious leader who can provide professional guidance and support. I think it's wonderful that today, more than ever, we are having an open dialogue about the importance of mental health and self-care. They are critical to our sense of safety, security, and well-being. Engage in activities that you enjoy and that bring you peace. Taking time for yourself can help rebuild your emotional strength.

Establishing new routines can help you move forward. Whether taking up a new hobby, joining a club, or volunteering, new pursuits can provide a sense of purpose and distraction when needed. Do things that fill your cup and make your heart sing. That's when you know you are on the right path. And if you're not yet at a point where your heart can sing, try to find out what makes it just a tiny bit happier.

I learned a great deal from my personal experience. When I reflect on my divorce from my husband, I find that I have garnered quite a bit of advice that I would offer to anyone going through a break-up. It may be difficult initially, but it can provide valuable insights into what you want and need in your life and future relationships. Recognize any patterns or behaviors that may have contributed to the break-up. Understanding these can help you make healthier choices in the future. In this time of reflection, I also think it is essential to take ownership of your shortcomings or contributions to the downfall of the partnership. That does not mean mentally or emotionally beating yourself up. An honest look at your choices can inform who you are and who you wish to become.

I do *not* recommend contacting your ex, at least not often and certainly not in the early days. Every time you engage with them, you run the risk of reopening that wound. The early days are about *self*-care. That means limiting contact with your former significant other. Give yourself space to heal. It can help you reduce your emotional turmoil and prevent prolonging your recovery. At the time of my particular breakup, we did not have social media, but these days, it is part of the fabric of our societal interaction. It is hard to put a person in your rear-view window when you see their picture or video popping up in your feed. Consider taking a brief break from social media or unfollowing your ex to avoid constant reminders that can hinder your healing.

One thing that was very helpful to me was reconnecting with myself. This time can be an excellent opportunity to remind yourself of who you are as an individual outside of a relationship. Explore whatever interests or passions you may have. You never know where they will lead. What is important is that you do things that make you happy. Choose to do things that build your self-esteem and remind you of your worth and value to others. Positive affirmations and achievements, no matter how small, can help rebuild your confidence.

Though reflection is good, wallowing in the past is not healthy at all. It's important to process what has happened, but looking forward to the future is equally important. Embrace the possibilities! What knows what lies ahead for you? Remaining optimistic will serve you well. You never know what fantastic new opportunities are waiting for you. Focus on the positive aspects of your life, and you will plant the seeds for more.

Though I have recommended taking a social media break, you don't want to take a long *social* break. Spending time with family and friends will help you feel less isolated and lift your spirits. When you feel ready, try meeting new people. It doesn't necessarily mean jumping into a new relationship, but expanding your social circle can be refreshing and provide new experiences.

Recovery is a journey, and everyone's story and timeline are different. Be patient with yourself and recognize that it's okay to have good days and bad days—we all do. Acknowledge and celebrate your progress, even if you're taking baby steps. Every step forward is a step toward growth and happiness.

As we are all unique, everyone has a different version of what self-care looks like. For me, it is traveling—*especially* (when I am fortunate enough to have the opportunity) traveling throughout Europe. Traveling became my self-care, and traveling-as-self-care completely changed my life.

Once I'd taken my time of introspection after my divorce and rebuilt my life as a single independent woman, I decided that I was going to go to Europe. I no longer felt I was running away. It was just what I wanted to do.

I'm glad I waited as long as I did for that trip for several reasons. Primarily, I'm glad I waited because I went to Europe with a new mindset. I stored my furniture, leased my house, and resigned from my job. Back then, you could not take a leave of absence from teaching. I had to resign and take what little money I had from my retirement account. I combined that with my savings and was able to make it work.

Bob and I lived with a German family when he was a private in the army.

The family, Mama and Papa Kertz, told me then, "On this side of the ocean, we are your Mama and your Papa."

My good friends Joanie and Don Roberts were also there. So, I had two bases there from which to travel. I planned to apply to teach in US military schools in Europe, and I did. I had an interview scheduled; however, coincidentally and unexpectedly, that was when French President Charles de Gaulle removed all French armed forces from NATO and sent US forces out of France. Suddenly, all the US military schools in France had to close, but all these teachers were under contract, so they had to be placed in other parts of Europe, Japan, or wherever there were schools for them.

I attended an interview with the superintendent of the Armed Forces Schools in Europe in Frankfurt. He was a delightful gentleman who knew I taught literature.

He said, "On paper, you're ideal. That's why I wanted the interview. But there's no way I can hire you. I have all these people that I have got to place." He thought for a moment, then continued, "One exception: If you can teach mechanical drawing, I'll chase you down with a butterfly net!"

I said, "Sir, I wish I could, but mechanical drawing is not one of my strongest fields!" And we laughed.

So, I needed help getting a teaching job. I had enough money to float for a year, but that was it. Not to be deterred, I decided to travel for the entire glorious year.

"I'm already here," I thought, "so I might as well make lemonade!"

I resolved that I had enough money saved to be "okay." My dear friends made it affordable and possible because I could stay with them and travel from their houses to various destinations. Sometimes Joanie, my best friend, would take a trip with me, and the Hausfrau would babysit the children. Don, her husband, was a thoracic surgeon and spent much time at the hospital, but sometimes, they'd join me together. We'd take a trip somewhere like Italy for a week. It was beyond fabulous! It may sound somewhat extravagant, but truly, travel was an exceptional form of self-care for me.

At the end of the year, I reapplied for a teaching position back home in Winston-Salem. I sent my application and cover letter to personnel in the Central Office. I sent copies to the superintendent, my principal at North Forsyth, Mr. Gibson, and the chair of the English Department, Mrs. Newman, who (as I have said) had been my teacher. I immediately heard back. I was rehired at the same school I had left the year before.

I had not told anyone I planned to return. I was thirty-four then, and unbeknownst to me, my life was about to change significantly.

Before I left Europe, I wanted to go to Scandinavia, but Joanie and Don couldn't, so I signed up for an American Express two-week tour of Denmark, Norway, and Sweden. The first part of the trip was from Frankfurt to Hamburg. At the bus depot, I ran into some people I knew. They weren't taking the tour, so I visited with them and was the last person to get on the bus. There was one seat left.

It was beside this gentleman, and I said, "Pardon me, sir, is this seat free?"

Sitting by the window, he rose out of his seat. He said, "Yes, ma'am, it is." I sat beside him, and he introduced himself, "I'm Ellis Dunning."

"I'm Phyllis Carswell," I replied.

I had no idea I'd just introduced myself to my future husband!

Ellis Dunning was originally from southern Alabama. He attended a military prep school in Alabama, the Marion Military Institute. Then, he enrolled at Auburn University, majoring in business for his ROTC (Reserve Officers' Training Corps). He graduated in 1937 as a second lieutenant in the army reserves. He married his college sweetheart, Marjorie, before being called to active military duty in 1941-42. He was in the army through World War II, and they had three children.

He left active duty at the war's end but stayed in the reserve. Following his father's footsteps, he opened an appliance and hardware business in Thomasville, Alabama.

Then, he was called back to the army during the Korean War. He and Marjorie decided that Thomasville, Alabama, was a lovely but small town, and they would like to experience life beyond that little town. They especially wanted their children to experience more of an international life. So, he sold the business and decided to stay in the army for his career.

They were stationed twice in Georgia, and in North Carolina, Oklahoma, Germany, France, and Washington, where Ellis had done ROTC at Georgetown University for three years.

After they were married twenty-nine years and the children were all adults and married, Marjorie became ill with cancer and died. A year and a half after she passed, he retired from the army, having thirty years of active service. He visited family and friends throughout the United States for about six months. Then, after six months, he went to Europe to visit his two children living there. His son, Bob, had gone to West Point. He and his wife and children lived in Heidelberg. Linda, his daughter, had married a military intelligence officer and lived in Frankfurt.

Of course, I didn't know any of his history then. I just knew I'd met a charming busmate who'd graciously agreed to let me sit beside him.

It was a trip where our hotels were booked in advance, but we were on our own to plan our sightseeing. For three or four days, Ellis and I sat together on the bus or across the aisle, and we were at the same table for breakfast several times. He was charming and engaging and could talk even more than I could, which is saying a lot! He had great stories.

Eight or ten days later, we were in Stockholm, and he said, "Now, Phyllis, there's something I want to do. I'm unsure how to do this because I have not done it in many years, and I'm not sure I'll get it right, but I want to ask you for a date."

"Well, I'd say you haven't lost your touch!" I laughed. "You've done a good job!"

I loved it. A friend had told him about a private club in Stockholm that was for dining and dancing and included a floor show with entertainment. So, off we went for an evening of cocktails, dinner, entertainment, and dancing. And that was our first date.

The tour was going to be over within another week. We exchanged names, phone numbers, and addresses, and the group agreed we'd all had a great time.

I remember thinking, "This has been delightful. He's interesting and very charming, and I wouldn't be surprised if our paths might cross again sometime."

I returned to Joanie and Don's house, and Ellis went to stay with his son, Bob, and daughter-in-law Carol in Heidelberg.

He called the next day! He said, "I have an idea. I would like to bring Bob and Carol and invite you and your friends, Joan and Don, to accompany us to the Officer's Club at Ramstein Air Base." It was near Kaiserslautern, Germany.

I said, "That sounds great. I'll check with Joanie and Don."

Joanie was onboard immediately.

After Joanie accepted, I said, "What if Don is on call?" (Don worked at the thoracic center for the military for all of Europe.)

Joanie said, "Well, Don will just have to get somebody to cover for him because we're going! I want to meet this guy."

It was an hour-and-a-half drive, and we met at Ramstein. I did not realize that Ellis had told Bob and Carol: "I want to pursue this. And I want you to see what you think. She's going back to the States within a month. If you approve, I would love for you to invite her to come to Heidelberg to be your houseguest for the weekend."

We had a wonderful evening, dining and dancing. You'd think everyone had known each other for years. Ellis and I rode with Bob and Carol from the Officer's Club back to Joanie and Don's apartment.

On the way, Carol—I can see her now—said, "I was just thinking, Phyllis, you're going to be leaving soon, and I know you've been to Heidelberg numerous times, but gosh, it'd be great if you could come at least one more time before you leave Germany. Why don't you think about it? We'd love to have you visit; maybe you could spend a weekend with us?" It was like she had just thought of it! Later, they all clued me in. That was the signal to Ellis that they approved: "Go for it!"

So, I went for a weekend, and it was wonderful. They had two delightful young children, Bob Jr. and Dana. We had a great weekend, and during our conversations, they asked when I was leaving Europe. I had to return to the states in mid-August so that I could resume teaching. I had planned to say my farewell to my year abroad by taking the train along the Rhine to the hook of Holland, where I would cross by ferry and take the train to London. I would spend eight or nine days there and go to the symphony, see some theater, and go sightseeing.

As we talked, Ellis said, "I was stationed in London during World War II, and when Marjorie and the children traveled to London, I was busy working and didn't get to go with them. It's on my bucket-list to go." He paused, "I don't want to intrude or impose, but it sounds like your plan is great. I would love to join you if you don't have anyone going with you."

I said, "No. It's just me."

And he said, "Well if you don't mind, what is your schedule?"

I told him my train and ferry schedules and where I was staying in London, and he got busy booking the same train and ferry, and checking into the same hotel.

We went out for dinner at Café Royale the first night we were in London. Wonderful. And, of course, I wouldn't let him pick up the check. Talk about an independent woman! I would never be obligated to anybody, and certainly not to some man I'd just met!

I insisted that I pay for my dinner, and later, back at the hotel, we stopped at the bar for a nightcap, and he said, "We need to talk. I am so uncomfortable with you paying for your dinner."

He wanted to attend the other activities I had planned, so I said, "Okay, maybe we can make a deal: If you pay for our dinners, I will pay for our tickets to the theater and music."

We were each on our own for breakfast and lunch. Often, I didn't see him until the afternoon. We might meet at five o'clock for a drink and then go out for dinner, or sometimes we'd meet somewhere for lunch, but we always split the check. He agreed to my proposal, so I went to the concierge and got two tickets to everything I wanted to see.

He, true to his word, bought dinner every night.

Ellis saw me off at Heathrow Airport, and when I arrived at Greensboro airport my Dad picked me up.

When we got home, Mother said, "Well, there were a dozen long-stemmed red roses and several phone calls from Ellis Dunning."

He was a full colonel by that point. He was fifty-three when I met him, nineteen years my senior. He had talked to Mother on the phone. Then he'd called again.

So, we met in July, I returned home in August, and he came to Winston-Salem in September. He'd planned to stay in Europe until after Oktoberfest but decided to return to the States early. It had been three years since Bob and I had split and three years since Ellis's wife had passed.

We married that Thanksgiving at Mother and Dad's house.

It was fast, given that it was the second marriage for both of us, and people are usually a little more cautious the second time. Bob and I were just so young—we were twenty and twenty-one at the time of our marriage. You just never know. You may think you are headed in the same parallel direction, but life has its twists and turns. It unfolds in ways we may not be able to predict. I read somewhere that you often marry the same type of person in a second marriage, but Bob and Ellis were so different. If there was ever a person who was committed and responsible, it was Ellis Dunning, the polar opposite of Bob in that way. Now, both were charming, likable, lovable, and popular. They both had that essence.

When, long after our wedding, Ellis and I would talk about commitment, Ellis used to say, "I was not looking to remarry."

I'd reply, "Ellis Dunning, if it hadn't been me, it would have been somebody else because you are such a married person!"

He'd laugh. "I'm so glad it was you." He liked to be married. We were very compatible and were together for over twenty years before he passed away.

I'm so grateful for those years and the time we had together. We had an excellent relationship, and I owe it all to that European trip. I might never have met my wonderful husband had I not taken the time for *self*-care and intentional living.

Life is full of beautiful surprises if you are ready to let them in. Do your inner work, then why not *learn how to dance in the rain?* I am forever grateful that I did.

LESSON 12

TRAVEL

The universe is a sort of book, whose first page one has read when one has seen only one's own country.

—Fougeret de Monbron

Since the preceding chapter on "self-care" heavily features the importance of travel in my life, I think it's only right that I include a chapter entirely dedicated to the subject. Education in the classroom is only the beginning; to be genuinely well-educated, nothing is as valuable as firsthand experience.

See it.

Feel it.

Taste it.

Touch it.

Everybody needs to travel. It is an integral part of the educational process. Everyone should experience different cultures, new languages, and foreign traditions and customs. When teaching, I encouraged my students to see as much of the world as possible. To entice them (and because I wanted to go on the trips anyway), I would whet their appetites through educational trips I hosted and chaperoned. It was a beautiful and memorable experience to travel with all of them. We came home with so many stories!

I did the same for my nieces, nephews, and grandchildren. I especially enjoyed exploring new locales with young family members, because I have found that young people are like sponges: thirsty for new experiences. I loved seeing them soak up every morsel of a trip. It was exhilarating to watch, and we created shared memories that we will carry with us throughout our lifetimes. My niece, Amanda, celebrated her sixteenth birthday in Europe, and my granddaughter, Dana, celebrated her seventeenth. Every moment of these trips was so very special to me.

Travel is enjoyable and rewarding, but *educational* travel can be totally transformative. It enriches students' learning experiences and improves their personal and academic growth. Given the advantage of learning in a real-world context, bringing their studies to life outside the classroom, students who travel learn at an accelerated pace. Seeing a historical place gives one a very different perspective than just studying it in a book, though, as you know, I am a strong advocate for both forms of learning. Books can open a world of possibilities if you cannot travel, and can supplement travel beautifully; the earlier chapter on "books" thoroughly explores these advantages.

Experiential learning, however, invokes a visceral response, an emotional attachment to a place that cannot be obtained from a book, no matter how well it is written. Whether visiting historical landmarks, scientific institutions, or cultural sites, educational tours offer hands-on learning experiences that deepen students' understanding of academic concepts and subjects. Students who travel are better able to grasp complex ideas and make meaningful connections. During one of our trips, my grandson, Jon, stood in the same place Caesar had once stood, and he was awestruck. Those kinds of moments have no price tag. They are life-changing.

These trips inspire a level of wonderment and excitement about learning that is beyond explanation. Exploring new environments, cultures, and perspectives ignites and stimulates a young person's intellectual curiosity. Whether exploring natural wonders, observing wildlife, or becoming immersed in different cultural traditions, these tours invoke a reverence in people that motivates them to explore, ask questions, and seek new knowledge. This excited curiosity enhances students' enjoyment of learning and encourages them to pursue further educational opportunities and academic interests. For example, my great granddaughter, Kait, accompanied me to London in her teenage years, and she was so enamored with the city that she returned to study there in her twenties. She warmed my heart when she fondly recalled her experience:

"My great grandmother is a woman of immense grace and sophistication who instilled in me a lifelong passion for travel, beautiful stationery, and the arts. Her captivating stories of adventures in distant lands ignited my imagination and sparked my curiosity about the world.

Like many others, I embarked on my first trip abroad with Phyllis, exploring the enchanting cities of London, Paris, Rome, and Lucerne."

Educational tours promote cultural awareness, empathy, and responsible global citizenship. This deeper understanding gives them a more inclusive and tolerant worldview. Mark Twain put it best when he penned the words, "Travel is fatal to prejudice, bigotry, and narrow-mindedness."

While participating in these tours, students also learn socialization, teamwork, and collaboration with their peers and grown-ups. Travel truly crosses the cultural divide of age and experience. It benefits a person's personal, social, and intellectual development. Bonds of lifelong friendship and camaraderie are forged as students share new experiences, overcome challenges, and support one another. They develop the skills, insights, and points of view necessary to thrive in an increasingly complex and interconnected world.

The first time I traveled with a group of students, I brought six students with me, and I hired a company called Scholastic Travel. The Scholastic Book Company had decided to add an educational component to their organization. I benefited from two fantastic trips with Scholastic. After two years, though, Scholastic decided to abandon their travel offerings and stick with selling books. I looked for another company and found the American Leadership Study Group (ALSG), a company out of Boston. I would take five to ten students on each trip, and ALSG would put my group with another group or two. So, if we were going from one city to another by bus, there would be an almost-full bus. We traveled with people from Connecticut, Oklahoma, California, Hawaii, Texas, and Florida. It was unforgettable.

After several years with ALSG (in 1976—the year that my granddaughter Dana joined us), a friend of mine who had also traveled with ALSG, Linda VanHuss, called me.

She said, "Phyllis, we want to start a touring company. We are three Brits and two Americans: Peter Jones, John Hannington, David Stitt, Michael Eisenberg, and me. Would you be interested in traveling with us?"

I said, "Linda, you have just named my favorite people! Of course,

I will travel with you all. Yes!"

"We call it ACIS," she told me, "the American Council for International Studies. We're starting this summer."

I said, "Sign me up!"

They put together a five-week package starting in London, and ending in Greece (sometimes Turkey). It's still a fabulous educational travel company. I went with them every year, and a couple of times I took two trips in a year. Compared to other companies, ACIS was more expensive, but we always stayed in hotels at the center of things, never out by an airport. The hotels would be three- and four-star hotels: small but adequate and suitable amid the center of activity. They were usually what would be called "boutique hotels." That's number one in importance when you're traveling on these trips: in Europe, you don't always have the level of accommodation you might find in America, and knowing that we would be adequately cared for in our accommodations throughout our journeys gave me peace of mind. When one is responsible for the well-being of minors, it is extra important to ensure the trip's details are "well buttoned up."

ACIS prided itself on its tour managers, who were always absolutely fabulous. They were not professional tour managers; they were usually either graduate students or postgraduates. They had to be well-traveled, well-educated, and multilingual, and they had to like Americans (not always a guaranteed quality in a tour guide!). Never patronizing or condescending toward American young people and their adult chaperones, these tour managers were good role models for our students. A quality tour manager and local guides are critical to creating a fantastic experience. Conversely, the experience can fall short of expectations and disappoint if they are not skilled at their jobs. But, I assure you, we were never disappointed!

Over the years, I have followed the careers of some of the guides we used. One of them, Simon Barrington Ward, eventually became a physician. He did not rush through the process to get there! Other guides we had became barristers and professors and (most importantly) friends.

One of the guides we used a lot was originally from Italy. He said,

"I will become a history professor and write history books," and that is exactly what he did.

Another guide, Jillian, became an actress.

Yet another, John Harrison, was a British architect who later came to the United States and studied landscape architecture. His sister and parents came from the United Kingdom to Massachusetts when he finished his studies there, and after graduation, they came to North Carolina to visit with me. His parents flew back to Boston and the United Kingdom when they left. John was going back as well, but around the world the other way, from here to California, to Hawaii, and onward.

My granddaughter Dana, grandson Jon, and their family were living in Hawaii at that time, so I alerted them by saying, "John Harrison, a young English architect darling, is coming, and he'll be arriving in Honolulu on [such and such a day]."

They met him at the airport with brightly colored leis, and he spent a couple of days there before flying to Asia.

I remember receiving a card from him from the Raffles Hotel in Singapore, which read: "Oh Phyllis, I had the most wonderful time in Hawaii! We met up with your granddaughter Dana and her friends. We went to the beach in Waikiki." He continued, "Do you have any relatives in Thailand, Iran, or Syria?" It was so cute!

When I took my family traveling, I always took them on educational trips. These were no pedestrian tours! They each chose five countries, and we traveled for five weeks. Later, I had to cut it to three weeks for monetary reasons. Three weeks today costs what five weeks cost in prior years. The shortest trips I took with my family (the most recent couple of trips), lasted eighteen days.

Granddaughter Dana also recalled her travels with me fondly. She wrote a lovely note saying:

"I'm in the middle of a crazy travel week and I'm reminded that it's really all Phyllis' fault! She inspired my love of this lifestyle! I have a quote on my wall by author Mary Anne Radmacher, acquired shortly after I started my career with Delta Air Lines. It simply says, 'Travel... I am not the same having seen the moon shine on the other side of the world.' Beautiful words with a powerful message that inspires me to this day.

My grandmother, Phyllis Dunning, has always been my cultural 'guru.' At seventeen, as an early graduation gift for me, Phyllis sponsored (and chaperoned!) an epic trip to Europe. This opened my mind and my world as she taught me how travel creates cultural experiences that fill your soul through art, music, history and exploration. This valuable lesson was a transformative gift given to me at an early age and fostered in me throughout my life. She continues to inspire and amaze and I feel grateful and blessed that we are family."

How blessed am *I* to have such a wonderful family?! Ellis' family embraced me as they would a blood relative from the time I came into his life and I have reciprocated. They are all wonderful human beings!

As I brought family, friends and students on various tours, I went to the same locations multiple times, but I certainly didn't care. I never get bored re-visiting travel destinations. I can handle Paris every summer for five days! I mean, come on, it's Paris!

Upon my return to big cities like London, Paris, Venice, Florence, Rome, or cities in Greece, we would stay in new hotels in various areas. For instance, our hotels would be in the heart of Venice. One hotel would be right at Piazza San Marco; another near the Gallerie dell'Accademia; another time, it would be a hotel on the other side of the canal across from the center of activity. Twice, we stayed in a hotel in Lido di Venezia. And in Paris, each neighborhood (*arrondissement*) is like a village unto itself. Sometimes, we stayed near Place d'Italie, other times near Place Vendôme, and other times in the Montmartre district or Île Saint-Louis. It was wonderful to stay in hotels in different parts of each city. With every visit, I reveled in a different flavor and experience.

We had local guides in each country and city, but our tour manager hired by ACIS always remained with us. They met us at the plane when we landed, joined us throughout the tour, and saw us off at the end of the trip.

I have to tell one more story about one of our tour managers: Paolo. When Paolo was our tour manager, he met us in London and accompanied us to Paris. When we got to Rome, we had this fabulous guide. She was a stunning, elegant woman who spoke English beautifully and was incredibly charming.

I remember walking alongside Paolo while we were following her somewhere, and I said, "Paolo, I've had fabulous guides all over the world, including in Rome, but never has anyone been better than this lady. And, by the way, in my next life that's how I'm going to look from behind! That's how I'm going to walk and move!" We enjoyed a good laugh over that.

After we had been in Rome for four days and were getting ready to leave, Paolo said, "Phyllis, I've got to tell you something I haven't mentioned: that lady is my mother!"

They had agreed not to mention their blood relationship if she were a guide for one of their tours, so that they would be treated more professionally.

I said, "That's amazing!"

Then, he told me about his divorced parents and his studies in England. He went to either Oxford or Cambridge. I can still see his mother in my mind's eye. They were amazing people.

The final tour manager I will mention was named Jillian. We talked one day, and I said, "Now, Jillian, what's next for you after we leave?"

She replied, "I'm going to do one more tour this summer, and then I am so excited about this fall because I'm going to be studying with the most fabulous professor." She raved about this person: "He goes to America and spends time teaching there yearly."

Many teachers do something like that. She continued chattering about how excited she was to study with him.

I don't know why I asked, but I said, "Well, he sounds fabulous! Who is this marvel of a man?"

"His name is Dr. James Dodding," she replied.

I was astonished.

"Jillian," I said, "the place in America where he teaches is the small city where I am from!"

I told her about the North Carolina School of the Arts and Wake Forest University. I knew Jim Dodding well. He was a remarkable person, a gifted pedagogue, and a fine human being. She was floored, and I was floored, too. Why I even asked her for his name, I don't know, but her enthusiasm for this person just sparked my interest. It is, indeed, a small world.

As my many stories about tour guides and managers I have known illustrates: traveling is an enriching experience that offers far more than just a change of scenery. It's a journey of personal growth that expands one's horizons and pushes one beyond one's comfort zone. Travelers develop a deeper understanding of themselves and the world around them.

When the world around you is different, you become different. We grow as individuals and as a society by broadening our mindsets and challenging preconceived notions. Interacting with people from all different walks of life gives access to a new vantage point from which to appreciate cultural diversity and embrace the beauty of our human differences.

As I discovered with my own experience when I went to Europe after my divorce, travel allows time for self-discovery and personal reflection. Stepping away from the routines and responsibilities of daily life provides the space to reflect on our values, aspirations, and priorities. Whether hiking through breathtaking landscapes, taking a walk on a tranquil beach, or simply gazing at the stars in a remote location, travel offers moments of introspection and self-awareness. These moments of solitude allow us to reconnect, gain clarity about our goals, and cultivate a more profound sense of purpose.

In the words of author David Mitchell, "Travel far enough; you meet yourself."

What more fantastic gift is there than really getting to know yourself? Some people live a lifetime and are unsure of who they are or what they want from life. Wouldn't you rather be curious than timid? We only get one life to live. Why not live it to the fullest?

Resilience and adaptability in adversity can be well-learned lessons through travel. Missed flights and lost luggage are inevitable. Don't let them deter you. These things can be worked out, and I promise your world will keep spinning. Language barriers and cultural misunderstandings are also things that travelers may encounter along the way. These experiences teach us to remain steadfast in adversity, adapt to unexpected conditions, and find creative solutions to overcome obstacles. Learning to navigate these uncertainties helps us develop invaluable life skills that serve us well beyond these journeys. Travel is a transformative experience regardless of our age or station in life. We ultimately emerge as more confident, adaptable, and empathetic people.

A phenomenal opportunity afforded to students today is studying abroad. What a fantastic program! I have yet to meet a person who has studied abroad who didn't gush with excitement about their experience. Studying abroad offers a wealth of benefits that extend far beyond the classroom. It enriches students' academic, personal, and professional lives, providing invaluable experiences and skills shaping their futures.

Studying abroad allows students to gain exposure to different teaching styles, perspectives, and areas of study. Whether attending lectures at prestigious universities, conducting research alongside esteemed professors, or engaging in hands-on learning experiences, studying abroad broadens students' academic horizons and stimulates intellectual growth. These cultural experiences enrich students' personal lives and enhance their ability to collaborate and communicate effectively on a global level.

Talk about personal growth and self-discovery! Living independently in a foreign country challenges students to navigate unfamiliar situations, overcome language barriers, and adapt to new surroundings. They become self-reliant and confident as they overcome obstacles and thrive in diverse environments.

One of the great benefits of studying abroad is that it enhances students' career prospects and professional development. In an increasingly globalized world, employers value candidates with international experience, cultural competence, and language proficiency. Studying abroad demonstrates initiative, adaptability, and cross-cultural communication skills, making students more competitive in the job market. Students can also do internships and pursue networking and professional development opportunities that enrich their resumes and broaden their professional networks.

Whether you study abroad, take an educational tour, or just hop on a plane and explore a new place, you will come back enriched.

For me, the best part about travel is the lasting memories. I have chosen to invest in my travels rather than a luxurious home. I always wanted to be "out there," exploring the beauty and richness of new destinations. That was my priority, and I loved every second of it. And though my home is not opulent, it is full of memorabilia and beautiful artifacts I have collected along the way. When I pick up something from one of my adventures, the essence of the place comes rushing back to me in Technicolor. Having shared that moment with others makes it even better.

And I cannot overstate how impactful traveling with my family has been. Exploring historical sites with family, too, creates lasting memories that they will cherish forever. Whether it's climbing the steps of an ancient pyramid, walking the halls of a medieval castle, or standing in awe before a world-famous monument, these shared experiences create bonds that strengthen family relationships and provide children and grandchildren with a sense of adventure and wonder. And the memories of these trips serve as a source of inspiration and joy, shaping children's worldviews and impacting their lives.

My family eloquently reminisced about their travel experiences during a dinner for my ninetieth birthday. Friends and family flew in from various states, and we had the most memorable reunion. As we sat around the table, the conversation turned to our shared travels. I had taken each of them on separate trips.

Grandson Jon said, "Certainly, the greatest joy that all of us got to experience with our grandmother was the European trips. What an adventure!"

His sister, Dana, said, "It opened our eyes and lives."

Jon spoke about life-changing moments: he visited London, Paris, Germany, Austria, Switzerland, and Italy. Dana visited London, Paris, Rome, Venice, Switzerland, and Greece on ACIS's first tour.

She said, "The trip was beyond memorable, but if I could do that again at age twenty-five or thirty, when my focus wouldn't be *entirely* on cute boys, I would!" We all laughed, and she acknowledged that she had still learned a lot.

My dear friend and Salem Sister, Susan Melville, a brilliant educator and stellar human being, also attended my birthday dinner with her wonderful husband, Charles. She asked, "Didn't you all grow up a lot as a result of these travels?"

They all agreed that they had. Susan added, "We saw it over and over again. The most immature kids that went on those trips grew up the most."

Jon responded, "When you travel, you realize that the world is not just your little town that you're from. It's the whole wide world that you've read about in books. That's the transformative part: you change."

Susan nodded, "Overnight. You change overnight."

Jon agreed, "You come back different." He recounted his most exciting moment: "I stood where Caesar stood! That was amazing!"

Dana said, "It was incredible how much we learned. It was not just fun. There was so much more to it. I became a flight attendant because of those trips." Dana is a beautiful, intelligent woman who has traveled the world many times throughout her career.

Great-granddaughter Kait agreed: "Definitely educational and life-affirming."

"That's what makes ACIS so great," said Jon. "It was an *educational* tour. It was all the things."

And sometimes, what was etched in their minds were the little moments we shared. Jon remembered, "Phyllis knew all the inside tips! 'Yeah, this is great,' she'd say 'but let's come and have a little coffee on the side over there.' Because she'd been there so many times, she knew the best stuff, and she had priorities!"

We all had a good laugh over that.

Then Katie Hall Nicolas, my wonderful Salem Sister who is fifty-two years my junior (yes, fifty-two!), chimed in. "What's your favorite kind of gelato?" she asked.

Of course, I answered: "Morning or afternoon?" Everyone laughed at the connoisseurship implied by this answer. "In the morning," I declared, "you must have peach or lemon—palate cleansers. Then, in the afternoon, I would mix some chocolate with hazelnut or something like that."

Kait replied, "And then Campari and cinnamon." I agreed wholeheartedly.

Susan chimed in, "I like them all!"

Dana finally confessed, "I don't like Campari. I wanted to because Phyllis liked it so much. It's elegant and very European, like the Aperol Spritz which is so popular, but I can't convince myself to love it."

But *I* really do. "In the evening, Campari, rum raisin." I said, "My good friend, Ella Fallie, is returning from Venice today. 'When you're in Venice,' I told her, 'go to Nico's for the best gelato. In Florence, go to Tivoli. They are the best ones.'"

"That's the best answer!" Katie decreed, "'What's your favorite flavor?' 'What time of day?' A lesson to be learned by all!"

Dana decided "Morning or Afternoon" should be written in calligraphy on a plaque on the wall. But Susan said, "You don't have to calligraph it. Get Phyllis to write it out because that handwriting is impeccable. You know when you've received an envelope from Phyllis. You don't even have to look at the return address." Good penmanship was a source of pride in my day. We practiced our handwriting for hours to get it just right. This may be an aside, but: even today, good penmanship says something about a person. Taking care to do any task is essential. It is your calling card. It speaks to your character.

Kait had a lot to say about penmanship: "Phyllis is the epitome of a perfect pen pal. The 'lost art' of letter writing was never lost on her. Receiving mail from her was always a delight, as I knew it would be filled with elegant letters or notes. Her graceful handwriting and carefully chosen stationery for each occasion fascinated me. I still cherish the memory of receiving my first monogrammed stationery from her for a childhood birthday—it made me feel so sophisticated, just like her!"

On the subject of travel, she said: "I have a memory of a great trip. I was sixteen, and my mom came with me. So it was Phyllis, my mom, a group of lovely folks, and me for our trip. We went to Paris, London, Venice, Florence, Switzerland, and Rome, which was *amazing*. It was my first time out of the country, and it was incredible. I was the only one of my sixteen-year-old friends who got to go to Europe. We learned so much. I think my mother and I were late for everything. That was my fault because my mother is very punctual. That was teenage me! As my husband knows, my timekeeping is not the best. Even though I was sometimes tardy, I remember that my favorite part was going to the Moulin Rouge with Phyllis!"

Jon chimed in: "Then afterward, you ended up living in London, going to school there, so the trip whetted your appetite."

Kait agreed, "That first trip had an impact on me. I thought I'd stay there for a while and see how my life would unfold."

Jon then looked at me earnestly and said, "Thank you for those indelible life lessons."

His sentiment says it all. I encourage you to travel. You will come back a new, refreshed, and wiser person.

LESSON 13

MINDSET

Change your thoughts and you change the world.
—Norman Vincent Peale

Besides travel, it is well worth our time to consider our inner world: our minds. How well do you know your mind? Phrasing it another way: do you know what kind of thinker you are? Thoughts lead to actions; actions change our lives. Delving more deeply into your mindset can inform you of your strengths and blind spots. Beyond being a positive thinker or a negative thinker, if you dive below the surface, you can learn much about yourself and reasons for the choices you have made. If you know yourself, you can become the architect of your thinking and, consequently, your actions.

Psychologist Carol Dweck discusses the concepts of a *fixed mindset* and a *growth mindset* in her book *Mindset: The New Psychology of Success.* These two mindsets represent vastly different attitudes toward learning, challenges, and personal development. A person with a fixed mindset believes their abilities, intelligence, and talents are static, unchangeable traits. In contrast, one with a growth mindset embraces the idea that abilities can be developed through effort, learning, and perseverance.

Shakespeare's works can teach us a great deal about this subject. Well-written fiction can sometimes make it easier to recognize psychological tendencies, as the characters can be deliberately crafted to represent archetypes in society. Though written centuries before these psychological terms were defined, Shakespearean characters capture the essence of these contrasting mindsets through their attitudes toward destiny, ambition, and change.

Shakespeare's tragic heroes often exhibit fixed mindsets, believing that fate, nature, or personal flaws bind them to a particular destiny. One notable example is Macbeth, whose belief in the witches' prophecy traps him in a deterministic worldview. Upon hearing the witches' predictions, Macbeth does not see opportunities for growth or change but instead becomes consumed by the idea that his future is preordained. His belief that he is "fated" to become king leads him to murder his friend Duncan, catalyzing his downfall. His famous aside in act 1, scene 3—"If chance will have me king, why, chance may crown me / Without my stir"—reflects his passive belief that his fate is fixed. His mindset leads him to view any attempt to change the course of his life as futile, resulting in his tragic demise.

Another character who exhibits a fixed mindset is King Lear. At the beginning of the play, Lear believes that his power, status, and identity are unchangeable. When he divides his kingdom among his daughters, he does so under the assumption that his authority will remain intact, even without his crown. Lear's inability to adapt or accept criticism, particularly from his daughter Cordelia, stems from his belief that his authority is a fixed aspect of his identity. His fixed mindset blinds him to the possibility of his fallibility, leading to his eventual madness and death. In act 1, scene 1, when he says, "Nothing will come of nothing," Lear reveals his rigid worldview, which cannot comprehend growth or change outside the established order.

In contrast, a growth mindset embraces change and development, the idea that intelligence, talents, and abilities can be developed over time through effort, resilience, and learning. People with a growth mindset welcome challenges, seeing them as opportunities to improve. They recognize that failure is not a reflection of their worth but rather a necessary step in the journey of self-improvement.

Shakespeare contrasts his fixed-mindset characters with characters who embody the growth mindset, showing that transformation is possible even in adversity. In *Henry V,* for example, Henry evolves from a reckless youth to a wise and practical king. His growth mindset is evident in his willingness to learn from his past mistakes and his ability to rise to the challenges of kingship. In the famous St. Crispin's Day speech (act 4, scene 3), he motivates his troops by reframing their struggle as an opportunity for greatness: "And Crispin Crispian shall ne'er go by, / From this day to the ending of the world, / But we in it shall be remembered— / We few, we happy few, we band of brothers." He transforms the adversity of being outnumbered into a source of strength, demonstrating his belief in growth through hardship.

Another character with a growth mindset is Viola in *Twelfth Night*. After being shipwrecked in a foreign land, Viola does not resign herself to her fate but instead adapts, disguising herself as a man to navigate her new circumstances. Her adaptability and resourcefulness are hallmarks of a growth mindset, allowing her to thrive in the face of challenges. Unlike characters with a fixed mindset who see their fate as sealed, Viola believes in her ability to shape her destiny. She takes control of her situation through quick thinking and resilience. As she reflects on the chaos caused by her disguise, she says, "O Time, thou must untangle this, not I. / It is too hard a knot for me t' untie" (act 2, scene 2). This line reveals her recognition that growth and resolution require patience and time, a characteristic of the growth mindset.

Shakespeare's works, filled with characters who either succumb to a fixed mindset or flourish through growth, offer timeless lessons about human potential. From Macbeth's tragic fall to Henry V's triumph, the mindsets guiding their actions profoundly shape their destinies. In the same way, adopting a growth mindset in our lives opens the door to continual learning, resilience, and the realization of our full potential. In contrast, a fixed mindset limits what we believe we can achieve. As Hamlet says to Rosencrantz (act 2, scene 2), "There is nothing good or bad but thinking makes it so."

Our mindset, like our fate, is shaped by the thoughts we choose to cultivate.

A student with a fixed mindset might avoid a complex subject like mathematics, thinking they simply "aren't a math person." This avoidance ensures they never improve, solidifying their belief in their limitations.

In contrast, consider Michael Jordan, one of the most celebrated athletes in history. He is often cited as a prime example of the growth mindset. After being cut from his high school basketball team, Jordan used the setback to fuel his desire to improve. Instead of seeing his initial failure as proof of his limited ability, he viewed it as an opportunity to work harder and refine his skills. His relentless commitment to growth, effort, and resilience helped him become a six-time NBA champion and one of the greatest players ever.

Jordan consistently pushed himself to improve, saying, "I've failed over and over and over again in my life, and that is why I succeed."

He turned moments of defeat into motivation. His growth mindset focused on learning from failures rather than being defined by them.

Knowing whether you begin with a fixed or a growth mindset is crucial for personal development because it shapes how you approach challenges, failures, and opportunities for improvement. Recognizing your mindset allows you to reshape your approach to learning and development actively.

You might ask, "How does one recognize and overcome limitations?"

Identifying a fixed mindset makes it easier to see where you might be holding yourself back. Do you tend to avoid challenges because you fear failure will expose your perceived inadequacies? This fixed mindset can lead to stagnation, because it limits your willingness to try new things or embrace opportunities that involve risk. Knowing that you can change your abilities through effort helps you push beyond the limitations of self-doubt. The sky is the limit for your potential to achieve whatever you dream up! There is no expiration date on learning or personal growth. A tweak in perspective can change your potential and your trajectory.

For instance, when you face failure, instead of interpreting it as a sign of inadequacy, what if you see it as a valuable lesson? Then, your world opens up to resilience, which is critical for long-term success in any area of life, from academics to career advancement, personal relationships, and emotional intelligence.

Understanding your mindset also impacts how you relate to others. A fixed mindset might cause you to view relationships or social skills as static, leading to frustration when conflicts arise or others don't meet your expectations. Conversely, a growth mindset encourages a more flexible and empathetic approach to relationships, acknowledging that people can change and grow. If you believe that personal traits like kindness or patience can be developed, you're more likely to work on improving those qualities in yourself and others. You can nurture better communication, problem-solving, and overall relationship dynamics from this vantage point.

Understanding the differences between these mindsets can also help cultivate a more profound love for learning. Embracing the growth mindset allows you to pursue new skills, knowledge, and hobbies without the fear of failure holding you back. This shift in perception opens up more opportunities for intellectual and personal exploration. It also reduces the pressure to be "perfect" from the start. Imagine how good it would feel to lift that pressure off your shoulders and become empowered to enjoy the journey of learning itself.

Knowing your mindset directly influences how you cope with adversity. A fixed mindset can lead to a defeatist attitude when things don't go as planned, potentially causing you to give up easily.

This is not to say that a fixed mindset is always inappropriate. There are instances where people with fixed mindsets have achieved remarkable success, particularly in fields that reward existing talents, early specialization, or environments prioritizing immediate results over long-term growth.

Though Michael Jordan eventually became a symbol of the growth mindset due to his famous persistence and resilience, he initially exhibited characteristics of a fixed mindset. In the early stages of his career, he relied heavily on his natural athletic talent and belief in his superiority over others. He struggled to accept constructive criticism or embrace teamwork. Instead, Jordan was known for his intense desire to win at all costs and his belief that his talent would be enough to lead his team to victory. Early in his career, he tried to dominate games on his own rather than focusing on improving his teamwork or adjusting his approach to fit his team's needs.

His natural talent and relentless drive propelled him to early success, including multiple scoring titles and individual accolades. However, he achieved true team success only when he began to work within a team dynamic under coach Phil Jackson and learned to trust his teammates, which reflects a shift towards a growth mindset later in his career.

Pablo Picasso, too, achieved tremendous success in art, and aspects of his journey reflect a fixed mindset that contributed to his achievements. He had an unshakable belief in his innate talent and artistic vision. From an early age, he saw himself as a genius and often dismissed the work of others as inferior. This conviction in his superiority gave him the confidence to push boundaries and develop revolutionary art styles like cubism, even when his work faced criticism or confusion from the public. Despite exploring multiple styles throughout his career, Picasso rarely doubted the value of his work. He firmly believed that his unique perspective made his art valuable and refused to significantly adapt to the changing tastes of audiences or critics. This focus on his artistic voice ensured his consistency and dominance in the art world.

While a fixed mindset is often associated with stagnation and an unwillingness to grow, these examples show that success can still be achieved in specific contexts where natural talent, early specialization, or a narrow focus on maintaining excellence can lead to exceptional achievements. However, it is essential to note that these successes come with limitations. A fixed mindset often restricts personal development, makes one less adaptable to change, and can lead to difficulty handling failure or collaboration. Many successful people, like Michael Jordan, have found that adopting aspects of a growth mindset later in their careers helped them achieve even more significant long-term success and fulfillment.

Once you've identified which mindset is more in keeping with who you are, how do you know what type of career would best match your personality?

People with a growth mindset thrive in careers that challenge them to learn new skills, adapt to changing circumstances, and continually improve. Conversely, those with a fixed mindset may prefer careers emphasizing stability, routine, and reliance on existing strengths without facing frequent challenges or changes.

Since I have seen many students grow and choose careers (and ask me for advice about career decisions), I would like to lay out some guides for what I think ideal careers would be for individuals with different mindsets.

Career Choices: Growth vs. Fixed Mindsets

Understanding your own mindset is crucial for both personal and professional development. It shapes how you approach the challenges, learning opportunities, personal and professional relationships, and moments to build resilience you will experience throughout your life. Recognizing whether you have a growth or fixed mindset can help you build habits and make conscious choices that align with your strengths and preferences.

Growth Mindset: A growth mindset is characterized by the belief that abilities and intelligence can be developed through effort, learning, and perseverance. People with this mindset embrace challenges, learn from failures, and continuously seek improvement. They thrive in dynamic environments that require adaptability and innovation. Ideal careers for growth mindset individuals include:

Entrepreneurship: Requires flexibility, resilience, and the ability to learn from failure while adapting to market changes.

Technology: Fields such as software development and AI require continuous learning and innovation.

Education: Teachers and instructional designers refine methods to meet diverse student needs, aligning with the growth mindset.

Healthcare: Professionals must stay updated on medical advancements and collaborate effectively.

Arts: Writing, graphic design, and filmmaking require creativity, experimentation, and resilience.

Consulting: Involves learning about various industries and offering solutions to unique challenges.

Engineering: Solving complex problems and improving designs aligns with growth-oriented thinking.

Marketing: A fast-paced industry that values staying current with trends and creating innovative campaigns.

Leadership and Management: Encourages innovation, collaboration, and team development.

Research and Development: Ideal for those driven by curiosity and experimentation.

Fixed Mindset: A fixed mindset is characterized by the belief that abilities and intelligence are static and unchangeable and that success reflects natural talent rather than only effort. People with this mindset often prefer stability, routine, and reliance on existing strengths, avoiding frequent challenges or changes. Ideal careers for fixed mindset individual's include:

Accounting: Involves established processes and procedures with less emphasis on creativity.

Administrative Roles: Offers stability and predictability with routine tasks.

Manufacturing and Production: Appeals to those who prefer consistency and fixed procedures.

Customer Service: Structured protocols for handling inquiries and complaints.

Data Entry or Clerical Work: Focuses on repetitive tasks with clear expectations.

Security Roles: Emphasizes reliability and adherence to safety protocols.

Technical Support: Troubleshooting within a defined framework.

Trades: Mastering established techniques in fields like plumbing or carpentry.

Human Resources: Structured environments for managing predefined systems.

Bank Tellers: Routine interactions and established banking procedures.

Choosing the Right Career Path

For a growth mindset, seek roles that challenge you to learn, adapt, and innovate. Embrace opportunities for continuous improvement and collaboration. For a fixed mindset, opt for careers that offer stability, routine, and opportunities to excel in well-defined areas.

Regardless of your mindset, success is achievable. While a fixed mindset may lead to early specialization and mastery in specific fields, adopting a growth mindset can unlock greater long-term success and fulfillment.

Final Thoughts: Your mindset is not set in stone. By recognizing and understanding your tendencies, you can cultivate a growth-oriented approach more actively. This shift in perspective opens doors to resilience, learning, and the realization of your full potential. Whether you choose a career that aligns with your current mindset or challenge yourself to grow, the key is to seize opportunities that enable you to thrive and make meaningful contributions to the world.

LESSON 14

THE ESSENCE AND IMPACT OF GIVING

Judge each day not by the harvest you reap but by the seeds you plant.

—William A. Ward

Life's rewards come in many forms, and some can be surprising. I am reminded of a song I learned in childhood: "Magic Penny" by Malvina Reynolds. As children, we don't often ponder the lyrics or meaning of songs. We sing along because they make us happy or everyone else is singing. It is not until we become adults that we understand their message. Seemingly straightforward, the concept offered in "Magic Penny" gives one much to ponder.

Love is something if you give it away,
Give it away, give it away.
Love is something if you give it away,
You end up having more.
It's just like a magic penny,
Hold it tight and you won't have any.
Lend it, spend it, and you'll have so many
They'll roll all over the floor...

The things that best feed our better impulses—being kind, caring, and loving rather than succumbing to our baser instincts and only trying to take—are a recipe for leading a happy, fulfilled, and purposeful life. They are also a perfect philosophy for supporting the arts, education, and your community.

Think of the many gifts your community has given you. A person's community can be pivotal in their personal growth and well-being. It provides support, resources, and a sense of belonging. Many people who have faced challenges such as job loss or health issues have been helped by community members who rallied together to offer assistance. A community can be a source of strength and much-needed guidance, whether through emotional support, sharing job leads, or organizing fundraising efforts.

Local organizations and groups can provide access to educational programs, workshops, and networking opportunities that empower and encourage people to develop new skills and enhance their career prospects. The encouragement and camaraderie within a community can positively impact a person's resilience, instilling a sense of hope and motivation that propels them to overcome obstacles and achieve their goals. Ultimately, a community's collective strength and solidarity can significantly enrich a person's life, making them feel valued and connected.

Doesn't that compel you to give back to your community? You can pay it forward to impact other people's lives in many positive and meaningful ways. Giving is a powerful and essential practice that benefits both the giver and the receiver. Sharing resources, time, expertise, and compassion is fundamental to human nature and a cornerstone of thriving communities. It transcends material wealth, since the resource given doesn't have to be money but can instead encompass acts of kindness, volunteerism, and support. The importance of giving cannot be overstated, as it plays a critical role in creating social cohesion, promoting individual well-being, and addressing societal challenges.

Many academic studies show that giving impacts mental health and overall well-being. Engaging in acts of kindness triggers the release of endorphins, often referred to as the "helper's high," which can improve mood and reduce stress. In the longer term, giving also provides a sense of purpose and fulfillment, enhancing life satisfaction. Knowing that your actions contribute to the well-being of others bestows a sense of meaning and connection to your broader community.

Philanthropy has long been considered one of the most noble and impactful ways to give back to society. It provides opportunities to support causes that reflect one's values and aspirations while contributing to positive change. Derived from the Greek words *philos,* meaning love, and *anthropos,* meaning humanity, *philanthropy* signifies a love of humanity and a desire to promote the welfare of others. Being a philanthropist involves more than just donating money; it is a broader commitment to positively impacting society. Philanthropists are vital in addressing social issues, sparking innovation, and creating a more equitable global community.

Before dismissing the idea that philanthropy is only for wealthy people, ponder the many charities and causes that rely on a myriad of small donations. Look at the crowdsourced fundraisers on platforms like Kickstarter, GoFundMe, Indiegogo, and DonorsChoose, to name a few. These fundraisers have significantly impacted people's lives, supporting their dream projects, getting them back on their feet after an illness or disaster, and more. And all of the results have been made possible through one small donation after another. More prominent donors move mountains in many ways, but without the army of small donors, many worthy causes would never come to fruition.

Philanthropy also plays a critical role in social justice movements. By supporting organizations that advocate for marginalized communities, philanthropists help to address systemic inequalities and promote human rights. This type of philanthropy can drive policy changes and shift public discourse, leading to more inclusive and fair societies.

Unlike *charity,* which typically focuses on immediate relief (and is also vitally important), *philanthropy* aims at long-term solutions and systemic change. It is *proactive* rather than reactive, seeking to prevent problems rather than merely alleviate symptoms.

I find supporting causes that promote access to education, especially in underprivileged areas, to be of utmost importance. Arts education is a particular passion of mine because of its transformative power in young lives. In a world increasingly dominated by technology, nurturing creativity through the arts provides balance and helps encourage the critical thinking necessary for a dynamic, evolving society.

Community programs focusing on reducing social inequality and creating inclusive spaces also appeal to me greatly. Empowering local communities with resources and opportunities that help them thrive strengthens society's fabric and leads to a more just and compassionate world.

Family values and upbringing play a crucial role in shaping philanthropic behavior. Those raised in families that prioritize generosity and community involvement are more likely to become philanthropists. Early exposure to acts of giving and the values of compassion and social responsibility can instill a lifelong commitment to philanthropy. Religious beliefs can also be powerful motivators for philanthropy. Many religious traditions emphasize the importance of charity and caring for the less fortunate. Tithing in Christianity, zakat in Islam, and dāna in Buddhism are all practices that encourage followers to give to those in need. In these traditions, philanthropy is considered a spiritual duty and a way to fulfill religious obligations.

As a former English teacher, I have to take a moment to reflect on philanthropic themes in literature. In his 1843 novel *A Christmas Carol,* Charles Dickens explores giving and compassion as the path to happiness and meaning in life.

> No space of regret can make amends for one life's opportunity misused.

Dickens reflects upon the moral redemption of the miserly Ebenezer Scrooge. Through his visits from the ghosts of Christmas past, present, and future, Scrooge learns that the rewards of generosity and compassion far outweigh the pursuit of personal wealth. His journey highlights the idea that giving to others offers a deep sense of personal satisfaction and fulfillment, a crucial reward for philanthropy.

Financial donations, especially in arts education and community development, nurture cultural enrichment, cultivate creativity, and generate opportunities for underserved populations. These causes have far-reaching impacts that reverberate across generations. As a donor, knowing that your contribution has catalyzed someone's creative journey, expanded their worldview, or provided them with opportunities they would not have had otherwise is immensely rewarding.

As a bonus, philanthropy can enhance one's social network, bringing donors into communities of like-minded individuals passionate about similar causes. These relationships can be a source of inspiration, collaboration, and continued personal and professional growth.

You might be reading my lengthy and passionate defense of philanthropy and still find yourself asking, "What is the value in supporting *arts* education and community programs?"

Arts education plays a vital role in shaping society by inspiring critical thinking, creativity, and cultural awareness. It empowers people, especially young people, to express themselves, develop self-discipline, and build problem-solving skills. Exposure to the arts broadens perspectives and nurtures empathy, two essential qualities for living in an increasingly diverse and interconnected world. For communities, investment in the arts contributes to cultural vibrancy and social cohesion, helping community members feel connected and part of a shared identity.

Despite these benefits, arts education isn't funded enough, especially in economically disadvantaged areas. Schools with limited resources are more likely to prioritize subjects like math and science, leaving arts programs to languish. This is why private donations and philanthropic support for the arts are crucial. Funding arts education ensures that all students, regardless of background, have access to programs that enrich their learning and provide them with well-rounded personal development.

Community programs, too, are essential to building a more inclusive and equitable society. From after-school programs to neighborhood revitalization projects, these initiatives promote social mobility and reduce inequality. They create safe spaces for learning, personal development, and community engagement and help address systemic issues like poverty, discrimination, and isolation.

Communal experiences create bonds of understanding and promote a sense of shared humanity, which is critical in a world where division can often seem more prominent than unity. Entertainer Bob Hope summed up the importance of giving with his sage words:

If you haven't got charity in your heart, you have the worst kind of heart trouble.

One of the organizations I choose to support is the Giannini Society. It was named after the first president of the North Carolina School of the Arts, Vittorio Giannini. The organization supports school programs, initiatives, and areas of immediate need. Indeed, I have been honored with a "Giannini Award"—I don't give lots of money (because I don't have lots of money), but I am a *consistent* donor, and I enjoy attending many events and have volunteered for many different and exciting projects related to the organization.

It is vital that we remember: small donations make a difference!

One of the initiatives I love to give to is the Pickle Pantry, which provides food for students at the North Carolina School of the Arts who can't afford food. As I've gotten older, instead of shopping for the food they need, I send them a modest check several times a year.

I have a friend, Danny Spillman, who does a lot for the school, and is an excellent example of how an individual's generosity can impact a community. He knows where to find food bargains, what students need, and what foods they like.

Occasionally, I've given Danny a check and said, "Danny, please go shop for me at the Pickle Pantry."

He is happy to do that. He's retired now, but he looks like a kid. I first met Danny when he was still teaching at Radford University in Virginia. I met him at a concert, and I would see him later at School of the Arts events. He would drive two hours from Radford to Winston-Salem to go to a performance—music, a play, whatever. After the performance, he would drive the two hours back home because he had to teach class the next day.

When he retired (about four years ago), after making the two-hour-trek for many years, Danny sold his house in Radford and built one near where he'd grown up in Belews Creek, North Carolina, near Walkertown.

I said, "Danny, I know you're building a house. You ought to move into *this* neighborhood near the School of the Arts. You're already at the School of the Arts all the time!"

If the wigs and makeup classes need male volunteers, Danny will say, "I'll be there." He'll often be their model or sit for them to make a wig. He's a virtuous and generous man.

In fact, Danny was at the ninetieth birthday celebration I previously mentioned.

I have a card from him that reads, "Now remember, anytime you need a ride anywhere, just text me."

In my later years, it is harder for me to walk, and he volunteers to take me to places like the symphony.

My dear friends and neighbors, Sandy and Bill Broadway, are usually the ones who pick me up to take me to the symphony, but if I'm going on a night that they are unavailable, I can call Danny. He'll drop me at the front door and park, then (after the performance has ended) he'll pick me up at the door. He is a gem. He "walks the walk," and I wouldn't have known him had it not been for our shared love of the arts.

> The best way to find yourself is to lose yourself in the service of others.
>
> —Mahatma Gandhi

This Gandhi quote makes me think of the many excellent causes one can champion and to which one can devote resources. I have some advice for anyone seeking guidance about which organization(s) they might want to support: choosing a cause or organization to give your time or your money to can be a profoundly personal decision. It requires reflection on your values, passions, and the kind of impact you want to have. For some, the choice is obvious; perhaps they have been personally affected by an issue or cause and want to give back in a way that resonates with their life experiences. For others, it may be a matter of researching and evaluating where their contributions can make the most difference.

Personal experiences, particularly adversity, can motivate people to become philanthropists. Those who have faced significant challenges, such as poverty, illness, or discrimination, often feel a deep empathy for others in similar situations. This empathy can drive them to help alleviate that suffering and provide opportunities for others that they may have lacked.

> To laugh often and much; to win the respect of intelligent people and the affection of children; to earn the appreciation of

> honest critics and endure the betrayal of false friends; to appreciate the beauty; to find the best in others; to leave the world a bit better, whether by a healthy child, a garden patch or a redeemed social condition; to know even one life has breathed easier because you have lived. This is to have succeeded!
>
> —Ralph Waldo Emerson

What organizations do you like? Which ones organically come to mind? I am drawn to organizations by their mission—if they elevate humanity or if they elevate a person's thought. I gravitate toward the ones that work with young people and relate in some way to the arts. I'm not against sports, but I think most sports are too violent. I don't care for that kind of competition. There are some beautiful strengths in sports, like teamwork, but to me, the arts civilize us. So, if I'm giving time or money, I tend to look toward education and the arts, and if you can tie those together, that's brilliant, and you'll be receiving my check.

You can research almost anyone's mission on their website. One of my favorite organizations is Authoring Action. I volunteer for them when I can. Their mission is impressive: "To transform the lives of individuals and the world through the power of creative writing, spoken word, visual and media arts, filmmaking, and leadership education that promotes positive systemic change." It creates "an opportunity for participation in the arts for youth and adults who would not ordinarily have the opportunity to discover their authentic voices through artistic development and/or who may lack one or more critical support systems."

Authoring Action is devoted to developing authors, community leaders, and advocates for social change—redefining learning through the arts and supporting more vital communities. I can't do much, but I support them however I can. Even a tiny donation is a lot to them, because, as I have said, small grass-roots donations add up. Now, Authoring Action has teamed up with my stellar former student Ben Folds's nonprofit, Keys for Kids, whose stated purpose is: "to provide young people in North Carolina who express an interest in learning to play piano but have limited opportunity with access to appropriate lessons and instruments at little or no cost...Keys for Kids will create a statewide network of arts partners providing free or affordable access to piano and keyboard education for school-age youth in North Carolina." Ben Folds and Authoring Action collaborate because they work with at-risk teenagers. Keys for Kids works through keyboard music and composing, and Authoring Action works with words. Isn't that an amazing, collaborative cause?

Ben credits early exposure to music as a child growing up in Winston-Salem as the impetus and inspiration for his creative journey as a professional musician. In his own words: "The reason I'm so enthusiastic and passionate about this initiative is that I believe our young people need, now more than ever, what music has to offer. Music is where we find harmony. It enhances our ability to learn, to communicate, and to be inspired in all facets of our lives."

Anything which elevates the mind—*that* is what is essential to support. It's arts, education, and especially *anything* geared toward young people (because they are the future).

Along with Authoring Action and Keys for Kids, I support many Winston-Salem organizations at various levels. Among my favorites are Salem College; School of the Arts; the Winston-Salem Symphony; Piedmont Opera; Old Salem; Reynolda House Museum; the North Carolina Museum of Art, Winston-Salem (formerly SECCA); A/perture Cinema; 40 Plus Stage Company; the Little Theatre; the Theatre Alliance; and the International Black Theatre Festival. There are many more as well. It all adds up if you give a little here and there.

I have also named several organizations in my will. Planned giving can significantly impact institutions and organizations. As the saying goes, you can't take it with you—but you can create a legacy and a lasting imprint on the world.

Have you taken time to think about your contribution to humanity? I would advise you to consider giving back. Giving back can set a positive example and inspire others to do the same. When people see the positive impact of community service, they are more likely to get involved. This ripple effect can lead to a culture of giving, where acts of kindness and generosity become commonplace.

Creating a culture of generosity requires intentional efforts to promote and normalize giving behaviors. Organizations and businesses can also help develop a culture of giving. Corporate social responsibility (CSR) initiatives, employee volunteer programs, and matching donation schemes can encourage a spirit of generosity among employees and stakeholders. By integrating giving into their core values and operations, organizations can contribute to the well-being of their communities and inspire others to do the same.

Education, too, plays a vital role in this process, as teaching, sharing and kindness to children can instill lifelong habits of generosity. Schools and families can encourage giving by involving young people in community service projects and charitable activities. By setting a positive example, you can encourage a broader movement towards civic engagement and social responsibility. What a priceless gift your actions can be!

Have you considered what it means to be a volunteer and what impact it can have on your community? It is an honorable act to offer your time, skills, and energy to support a cause without expectation of monetary compensation. Volunteers are angels on earth. They are driven by a desire to make a positive impact and contribute to the well-being of others. Volunteering encompasses various roles and can occur in diverse settings, from local communities to international projects, but should ideally spring from selflessness and altruism. This selflessness is rooted in the belief that contributing to the greater good is a valuable and fulfilling endeavor, and from empathy, compassion for others' struggles, and a desire to alleviate suffering and improve lives. Volunteers are typically passionate about the cause they support: environmental conservation, education, health care, animal welfare, social justice, and so on. This passion drives their dedication and efforts.

People working toward common goals help build social networks and strengthen community ties. This form of civic engagement empowers people to contribute by actively addressing local and global challenges.

Effective volunteering requires a commitment to show up and fulfill responsibilities consistently. Those who "show up" really show up. Other people count on them. Volunteering also requires flexibility and a willingness to adapt to different tasks and environments. Volunteers can engage in various activities, from hands-on tasks like building homes or cleaning parks to specialized roles like tutoring, mentoring, or legal advice. They must also be open to new experiences and challenges. And by rising to meet those challenges, volunteers often acquire new skills. These can range from practical tasks like event planning and fundraising to soft skills like communication, teamwork, and leadership. These types of activities evoke a sense of accomplishment and fulfillment. Knowing one's efforts have positively impacted can enhance self-esteem and overall life satisfaction.

A volunteer makes a tangible difference. They contribute to meaningful change by addressing immediate needs and supporting long-term projects. Their efforts can improve the quality of life for individuals and communities and help build a more just and equitable society. They play a critical role in the operations of nonprofit organizations, helping them achieve their missions and expand their reach and impact.

Ultimately, philanthropy and volunteerism are about harnessing the power of human kindness and ingenuity to create a better world for present and future generations. The rewards of giving back are immediate and resonate far beyond one's lifetime, leaving a legacy of positive influence.

Wouldn't you like to be a part of shaping a better future? What is it that drives you to want a better world? What are your passions? What type of change would you like to see? With both philanthropy and volunteerism, the potential for positive change is immense.

LESSON 15

LIFE IMITATING ART, IMITATING LIFE: A SHAKESPEAREAN PERSPECTIVE

The purpose of playing . . . both at the first and now, was and is, to hold, as 'twere, the mirror up to nature.
—William Shakespeare, *Hamlet,* act 3, scene 2

As you can probably infer from my mentions of Shakespeare in previous chapters, I have long been an ardent proponent of Shakespearean plays. After all, he didn't write any duds! Shakespeare's language is poetic and rich in imagery, but more importantly, we can learn so much about life through his characters and their situations. Many people are intimidated by Shakespeare because his language sounds foreign to modern ears. However, taking the time and thought to decode and ponder this language is well worth one's time.

Shakespeare's exploration of life imitating art imitating life underscores the long-standing relevance of creative expression. His works illuminate the human experience and challenge us to confront our beliefs, aspirations, and shortcomings. As we navigate the complexities of our lives, Shakespeare's timeless wisdom continues to guide and inspire, reminding us that the lines between art and life are fluid and intertwined—a testament to the enduring power of storytelling and its profound impact on the human spirit.

As we have all observed, the boundaries between art and life often blur, with each reflecting and influencing the other in profound ways. Shakespeare famously captured this phenomenon in his plays, which serve as a testament to the interconnectedness of creative expression and human experience.

The unparalleled bard of Avon masterfully wove narratives that not only mirrored the societal norms and dilemmas of his time but also delved into universal human truths that resonate across centuries. Take, for instance, *Hamlet,* where the title character's existential crisis mirrors the doubts and complexities faced by those grappling with moral decisions and familial obligations. Hamlet's famous "To be, or not to be" soliloquy encapsulates the enduring struggle of existence, compelling the audience to reflect on their lives and choices. Similarly, in *Romeo and Juliet,* Shakespeare portrays the intensity of youthful passion and the tragic consequences of familial strife. The play's depiction of love, loyalty, and fate speaks to the human condition, resonating deeply with audiences who have experienced the tumultuous journey of love and its obstacles.

However, Shakespeare's genius goes beyond mere reflection; his works also anticipate and shape societal norms and cultural attitudes. The exploration of power dynamics in *Macbeth* or examination of gender roles in *Twelfth Night* did more than mirror Elizabethan society. They also challenged and influenced perceptions that continue to reverberate in contemporary discourse.

Consider the adage "All the world's a stage" from *As You Like It.* This underscores the performative nature of human interactions, reminding us that societal expectations and personal ambitions often influence our actions and personas. Just as actors assume roles on stage, people navigate various roles and identities in their professional, social, and personal lives, adapting to different scripts and contexts.

Shakespeare's portrayals of human emotions—love, jealousy, ambition, despair—resonate because they capture the complexities and contradictions of the human psyche. These themes reflect our own experiences and prompt introspection. When we witness characters like Othello succumbing to jealousy or Lear grappling with pride, we recognize facets of ourselves in their struggles and triumphs. Shakespearean drama reminds us of the transformative power of storytelling itself. Through art—literature, theater, music, or visual arts—humans transcend their immediate circumstances and find solace, inspiration, and understanding. Just as Shakespeare's plays continue to captivate and enlighten audiences worldwide, art in its myriad forms serves as a mirror that reflects and shapes our collective consciousness.

Shakespeare and other artists have longevity thanks to their ability to view society and culture in an insightful way that is, despite the time of its creation, familiar to us. It allows us to step outside our lives and see emerging themes more clearly when played out in other people's lives. This is a significant part of what makes such work and storytelling transformative.

Let's look more closely at the famous lines I have just referenced from *As You Like It* (act 2, scene 7):

> All the world's a stage,
> And all the men and women merely players.
> They have their exits and their entrances,
> And one man in his time plays many parts,...

These words carry profound implications for our daily lives, encouraging contemplation of our roles as parents, professionals, partners, friends, or citizens. These are not rigidly defined but rather performative, meaning that we actively shape and embody them through our actions, attitudes, and interactions. Understanding the performative nature of these roles allows us to navigate them more consciously and effectively.

Each role exists within specific contexts and comes with expectations, responsibilities, and behaviors. For example, the behavior expected of us as professionals in a corporate boardroom may differ significantly from expectations of us as parents at a school event. Awareness of these contextual differences enables us to adapt our behavior accordingly while staying true to our core values.

Conscious role navigation involves intentionality. Rather than simply reacting to situations, we proactively consider how our actions contribute to the fulfillment of our responsibilities and the well-being of others. As parents, this might mean consciously spending quality time with our children, actively listening to their concerns, and providing guidance based on their developmental needs and personalities.

Shakespeare's metaphor prompts us to be mindful of the authenticity of our actions and identities. Are we genuinely expressing ourselves or merely conforming to societal expectations and norms? It encourages us to strive for authenticity in our interactions and decisions, recognizing that while we may play roles, our true essence lies beneath the surface. Living consciously also means committing to continuous learning and personal growth. It involves seeking feedback from others, reflecting on experiences, and actively seeking opportunities to improve our skills and understanding. It might mean staying informed about social issues, participating in community activities, and advocating for positive change.

If you are interested in the relevance of Shakespeare's words to your everyday life, you may ask yourself: what practical strategies can I adopt to consciously navigate the various roles that I play? I have given this some consideration, and have come up with some approaches that may be helpful:

Regularly reflect on your roles and how they align with your values and goals. If they do not align with your values or make you uncomfortable, find alternative ways to navigate your environment.

Practice open and honest communication. It brings clarity and mutual understanding in relationships and professional settings.

Establish boundaries to help manage expectations and balance responsibilities effectively.

Prioritize self-care (which I have mentioned) to maintain well-being and sustain energy levels necessary for various roles.

Understanding that our societal roles are *performative* empowers us to navigate them with mindfulness, purpose, and authenticity. By approaching each role with awareness of context, intentionality in actions, and a commitment to growth, we enrich our own lives and contribute positively to the lives of others and the communities we are a part of. This conscious navigation cultivates deeper connectivity, enhances personal fulfillment, and promotes a more harmonious and meaningful existence.

Circumstances change, and roles evolve. With flexibility, we can respond to new challenges, adjust our approaches, and learn from our experiences. As partners, we might adapt to changes in our significant other's needs or life circumstances and find new ways to nurture the relationship. In our daily lives, whether with partners or others, we are intricately interconnected with others in ways that often surprise and reveal profound coincidences. These connections underscore the shared experiences and interwoven destinies that shape our interactions and understanding of the world. It's common to unexpectedly meet someone who shares mutual friends or interests or has crossed paths with us in unexpected places (as I have done and have described in previous chapters). Sometimes, we discover that a person we know has had experiences that are parallel to ours. They've faced similar challenges or milestones despite having a different background or circumstance.

We have all shared ideas or perspectives with others that seem remarkably aligned despite not having discussed them previously. There are many examples of this in my own life's narrative, as I have mentioned previously: I have met like-minded strangers through travel or work who have become good, lifelong friends.

Recognizing that everyone plays their part on this stage of life elicits empathy and understanding. We realize that each person we encounter is navigating their roles, facing challenges and triumphs. This awareness promotes much-needed compassion in today's society as we appreciate the complexities and diversity of human experiences.

Pondering the nuances of "All the world's a stage . . ." invites contemplation on the purpose and meaning of our lives. Like characters in a play, we contribute to the broader narrative of today's society and history. We must consider how our actions and choices benefit the greater good or impact those around us. Shakespeare wisely recognized the interconnectedness of humanity. We all play various roles in the grand theater of life, interconnected by our shared experiences and roles. Ultimately, Shakespeare's metaphor reminds us that life is a dynamic and evolving performance, and our ability to navigate its stages with grace, humanity, and purpose enriches our own lives and the lives of others.

O, it is excellent
To have a giant's strength, but it is tyrannous

To use it like a giant.
—*Measure for Measure,* act 2, scene 2

Possessing power or influence (whether physical, social, or moral) comes with responsibility. Shakespeare warns against using that power carelessly or oppressively, acknowledging how actions, especially those of people in positions of authority, can profoundly affect others.

Flexibility and awareness of the consequences of our choices play critical roles in shaping our own experiences. This awareness allows us to adapt to and learn from changing circumstances. We are all works in progress, and we are all fallible. Awareness of how our actions impact others reminds us to consider the outcomes and adjust as needed.

Uneasy lies the head that wears a crown.
—*Henry IV,* Part 2, act 3, scene 1

In this passage, King Henry IV weighs the burdens of leadership. Despite the outward appearance of rarefied privilege and absolute authority, the ruler's life is filled with anxiety, difficult decisions, and the weight of responsibility for the well-being of the entire kingdom. Shakespeare uses this line to convey the truth that power often comes at the cost of personal peace and happiness. The implication of the passage is that, although it is not always an easy burden to shoulder, we must sometimes "step up," and assume important responsibilities.

Give thy thoughts no tongue,
Nor any unproportioned thought his act.
Be thou familiar, but by no means vulgar.
—*Hamlet,* act 1, scene 3

Here, Polonius advises his son Laertes to be *mindful* of his words and actions, illustrating the importance of thoughtful consideration before speaking or acting. To be mindful, as was noted in the chapter on mindfulness, is also to acknowledge the impact of our choices and behaviors.

What's done cannot be undone.
—*Macbeth,* act 5, scene 1

With this simple statement, Lady Macbeth recognizes the irreversible consequences of her actions. It is essential to consider repercussions before acting. Mindfulness involves owning up to mistakes, fulfilling commitments, and striving to make amends when necessary. It might include sincerely apologizing when we hurt someone's feelings and taking steps to avoid repeating such behavior.

Our remedies oft in ourselves do lie
Which we ascribe to heaven.
—*All's Well That Ends Well,* act 1, scene 1

In this excerpt from *All's Well That Ends Well,* Helen recognizes that we often hold the power to change our own circumstances, and we need not attribute the beneficial outcomes of our own actions to external (even supernatural) forces.

There is nothing either good or bad but thinking makes it so.
—*Hamlet,* act 2, scene 2

This quotation appears to be straightforward: perception is subjective. Hamlet suggests that our thoughts influence how we interpret and respond to events. Mindfulness helps us observe our thoughts without immediately judging them, promoting clarity and wise decision-making. Expanding our emotional intelligence, we tap into our intuition and resilience. These principles form the foundation of ethical behavior, guiding us to act with integrity and accountability in all aspects of life.

Leaders who embody mindfulness and responsibility inspire trust and respect, build a positive organizational culture, and promote collaboration and innovation. Incorporating mindfulness and taking responsibility for our actions enhances our ability to navigate life's challenges with clarity and integrity. Shakespeare's timeless wisdom provides profound insights into these concepts, reminding us of their enduring relevance in shaping our character and relationships.

> This above all: to thine own self be true,
> And it must follow, as the night the day,
> Thou canst not then be false to any man.
> —*Hamlet,* act 1, scene 3

In this passage, Polonius advises his son Laertes to prioritize *authenticity* and *integrity*. He emphasizes the importance of being true to oneself as a foundation for honest interactions with others.

Authenticity and integrity are fundamental principles that guide our actions, decisions, and interactions with others. They are closely related but distinct concepts that reflect our character and ethical conduct.

Authenticity refers to being true to oneself, genuine, and sincere in thoughts, words, and actions. It involves *self-awareness*—understanding one's values, beliefs, strengths, weaknesses, and emotions; *consistency*—acting in alignment with one's true beliefs and values across different situations and contexts; *transparency*—being open and honest about one's thoughts, feelings, and intentions with oneself and others; and *acceptance*—embracing imperfections, vulnerabilities, and unique qualities without pretense or facade. Authenticity allows us to cultivate deeper relationships with others based on trust and mutual understanding. Self-acceptance leads to personal growth and the courage to live according to our convictions, even when faced with challenges or societal pressures.

Integrity, on the other hand, is the adherence to moral and ethical principles, honesty, and consistency in actions, regardless of external influences or circumstances. Critical aspects of integrity include *honesty*—being truthful and sincere in communication and interactions, avoiding deception or manipulation; *ethical decision-making*—making choices based on moral principles and values, even when difficult or unpopular; *reliability*—fulfilling commitments, responsibilities, and promises to oneself and others; and *accountability*—taking ownership of one's actions, accepting consequences, and learning from mistakes. Integrity is about having a strong moral compass and demonstrating reliability and trustworthiness in all aspects of life. It builds credibility and respect for oneself and others, forming the foundation of ethical leadership and meaningful relationships.

> Mine honor is my life; both grow in one.
> Take honor from me and my life is done.
> —*Richard II,* act 1, scene 1

Here, Thomas Mowbray equates honor and integrity with life itself, suggesting that life has no meaning without honor. The implication of this passage is that a life lived *without* honor (a life without the willingness to fulfill obligations, keep agreements, and adhere to what one believes is *right*) is not truly a life worth living.

> No legacy is so rich as honesty.
> —*All's Well That Ends Well,* act 3, scene 5

This quotation reflects the value of honesty as a lasting personal trait. Striving for authenticity in our actions and identities involves aligning our behaviors and expressions with our true beliefs and values. Furthermore, our reputations and the impressions we leave behind as we navigate our lives is only enriched and enhanced by a dedication to behave honestly.

> We are such stuff
> As dreams are made on, and our little life
> Is rounded with a sleep.
> —*The Tempest,* act 4, scene 1

Here, Prospero speaks of the transient nature of life and the universal human experience. Despite our independent paths, we share our humanity. Understanding this invokes empathy. We recognize that the joys, struggles, and aspirations of others resonate in our own experiences.

This realization promotes compassion and a deeper appreciation for the diversity of human perspectives and circumstances.

The quality of mercy is not strained.
It droppeth as the gentle rain from heaven
Upon the place beneath.
—*The Merchant of Venice,* act 4, scene 1

This quote speaks to the universal need for compassion and understanding, emphasizing that mercy and empathy should flow naturally from our shared humanity.

This bud of love, by summer's ripening breath,
May prove a beauteous flower when next we meet.
—*Romeo and Juliet,* act 2, scene 2

Shakespeare's depiction of young love in *Romeo and Juliet* illuminates the transformative power of understanding, as Romeo and Juliet's connection transcends their families' feud.

We know what we are but know not what we may be.
—*Hamlet,* act 4, scene 5

We are reminded of the potential for growth and transformation in our lives. Our actions can lead us to unexpected and meaningful outcomes.

How far that little candle throws his beams!
So shines a good deed in a naughty world.
—*The Merchant of Venice,* act 5, scene 1

Even small acts of kindness and generosity have a significant impact. Their ability to uplift others can be powerful beyond measure.

The better part of valor is discretion, in the which better part I

have saved my life.
—*Henry IV,* Part 1, act 5, scene 4

Shakespeare emphasizes the importance of wise and thoughtful actions. Prudence and discernment can lead to positive outcomes for oneself and others. By finding purpose and meaning in our daily lives and contributing to the greater good, we enrich our experiences and positively impact the world.

Shakespeare's sage insights encourage authenticity, self-discovery, and a commitment to making a difference, inspiring us to strive for personal fulfillment while contributing to a more just and compassionate society.

LESSON 16

THE JOYS AND NECESSITY OF HUMAN CONNECTION

I knew it not good for man to be alone.
—John Milton, *Paradise Lost*

I am blessed to lead a fulfilling and active life. On any given week, my calendar is packed with activities. Whether I'm taking in a performance of the symphony, opera, or School of the Arts; enjoying book club, church activities, and community events; or joining friends for lunch, dinner, or a glass of wine: I have plenty to do! It was my plan, when I turned eighty (over a decade ago now), to relocate to Arbor Acres, the beautiful continuing-care retirement community where many of my friends have moved in their later years. Arbor Acres is a picturesque neighborhood with a vibrant spectrum of social activities. When I look at my calendar, however, I don't know where I would fit these vibrant social activities in!

It has been many years since my beloved Ellis passed away. Of course, I miss him and our fabulous life together, but I have found many exciting ways to live life to the fullest. Sadly, many other people have not had this type of rewarding experience. Too many people face isolation and loneliness daily.

If you are in good health, going out and touching the world is essential! If you have health restrictions, figure out a way to work within the parameters of your abilities. We all need community! If you feel lost or forgotten, you need your community more than ever. If you can't get out to experience community, find a way to bring your community to you.

Human connection is essential for emotional and physical well-being. We are social beings who thrive on interaction with others. We are hardwired to form relationships and create meaningful bonds. This desire for connection is not just an emotional luxury, it is deeply embedded in human biology and psychology. We have an innate need to *belong.* When we connect with others, we experience support, understanding, and shared experiences vital to our emotional health.

This need is so strong that the absence of social interaction can lead to serious mental and physical health issues. Conversely, strong human connections can contribute to longevity, emotional stability, and overall well-being.

When people engage with others through close family relationships, friendships, or community involvement, they experience a sense of validation and acceptance. These connections provide a safe space for sharing feelings, alleviating worries, and celebrating joys. They provide comfort during difficult times and can boost self-esteem, encourage personal growth, and enhance overall life satisfaction.

Sharing challenges and burdens helps to distribute one's emotional load. Talking through problems can help people gain perspective and feel less isolated. This reduction in perceived stress can lower the risk of mental health disorders such as depression and anxiety. People who maintain close relationships are more likely to have a stronger sense of purpose and identity, which can act as a buffer against these feelings of loneliness and depression.

Human interaction is fundamental for good physical health as well. Scientific research has consistently shown that people with strong social connections live longer and healthier lives. One of the primary reasons for this is the impact on the body's stress response. When people are socially connected, they experience less chronic stress, which is known to contribute to health problems including high blood pressure, heart disease, and weakened immune function. The presence of supportive relationships can help regulate the body's stress hormones, such as cortisol, reducing the wear and tear on the body.

People who are part of a community or have close relationships are also more likely to make healthier lifestyle choices—to engage in regular exercise, maintain a balanced diet, and avoid harmful behaviors such as smoking or excessive alcohol consumption. Indeed, married couples live longer, on average, and have fewer health problems! This is, in part, because they encourage each other to maintain healthy habits.

Isolation, on the other hand, can lead to the deterioration of both emotional and physical well-being. It can contribute to feelings of worthlessness, despair, and hopelessness, which may result in a downward spiral of mental health issues. People who experience chronic loneliness are at a much higher risk of developing mental health disorders, including depression, anxiety, and cognitive decline.

Babies have an innate need for connection and human touch. Touch is critical in their physical, emotional, and cognitive development and is fundamental in building secure attachments between them and their caregivers. Skin-to-skin contact, such as holding or cuddling, releases oxytocin (the "love hormone"), giving babies a sense of safety, love, and trust. This bonding is essential for their emotional well-being and security.

Touch stimulates the development of the baby's brain and body. Babies communicate through touch long before they can use language. Holding, stroking, and touching help them interpret the world, learn social cues, and understand affection and social interaction. Touch provides the nurturing warmth and security essential for a baby's well-being.

We adults can learn a lot from babies. The need to connect is natural from the moment we enter this world. In today's fast-paced, digital world, where face-to-face interactions are often replaced with virtual connections, prioritizing building and nurturing relationships is *essential.* It can be easy to overlook the importance of meaningful human contact, but we need it now more than ever.

There are many ways to connect with others. We can strive to maintain existing relationships with family and friends if those relationships are healthy. During the COVID-19 pandemic, we learned a lot about the importance of familial and friendly ties as a society. Remember how much we all craved personal interaction? It is a human *need.* Making time for regular communication and in-person exchanges takes effort, but the rewards are unparalleled. Simple acts like sharing meals, walking, or engaging in meaningful conversations can strengthen these precious emotional bonds.

Engaging in community activities like the ones I have mentioned earlier (volunteer work, joining clubs, or participating in social events) is also extremely beneficial. Being part of a group with shared interests (like my book club!) provides that sense of belonging and purpose we all crave. It also creates opportunities to meet new people. Building a support network and leaning on it during difficult times can significantly improve your ability to cope with stress and maintain robust mental and physical health. Seeking help in times of struggle is paramount. Invest time and energy into relationships. You will reap the rewards of better mental and physical health and live a more connected life.

I will share a secret about how I facilitate social connections: when I meet interesting new people, I always give them my calling card! Yes, I have beautiful, embossed calling cards, even at my age. They simply state my name and contact information. I have found them to be very useful (one should always be prepared to make new acquaintances)! You never know when you'll encounter someone you might want to spend more time with. We could exchange numbers electronically using our phones, but, in my opinion, that tends to "break" the moment. Plus, a calling card says something more about you: you care about details and personal touches. I believe that it's essential to make a good first impression. You may not have the opportunity for a second encounter. And when a ninety-year-old woman passes you her calling card, that makes a lasting impression!

I often invite whomever I've just met to the symphony, a School of the Arts performance, the opera, or whatever is happening in town at that time. People appreciate the invitation, and many have become avid patrons of our thriving arts scene in Winston-Salem. People often just need exposure and a little encouragement to get involved. Once they do become engaged, a magical symbiotic relationship with the arts, artists, and friends they meet while attending events will likely blossom. I champion our many arts organizations because I understand their importance to the fabric of our community and because I am enamored with nurturing people's God-given talents. Exposing new people to the wealth of talent in our fair city of Winston-Salem is always a thrilling experience.

My dear friends Frank Benedetti and Gary Trowbridge are a darling couple who recently celebrated sixty years together; I met them because we happened to be seated next to each other at a performance of the Winston-Salem Symphony years ago. We happily chatted before the curtain went up, and of course, I gave them my card. I invited them to be my guests to the Magnolia Ball, a magnificent annual gala benefiting the Piedmont Opera. As a fundraising joke, I told them admission was free, but it would cost them a thousand dollars to get out! They had a wonderful time, made new friends, and have been avid supporters of our opera ever since. This past year, they were honored at the Magnolia Ball for their dedicated service. They always joke about their philanthropic journey that they were rich before they met Phyllis Dunning. We have had many good times together, and they are favorites among our opera-going community. Had I not given them my card and pursued our relationship, we would have missed-out on many invaluable shared memories.

One of the greatest pleasures of networking is making introductions between people who would otherwise never meet. These moments often feel like small acts of serendipity—an introduction at a party or a coffee meeting that leads to deep friendships or fruitful professional collaborations. I love connecting with new people, young and old. I love exposing them to new opportunities and introducing them to the arts, and I especially love introducing them to each other. I know so many extraordinary people who would be great friends—they just don't know it yet!

This book, for example, would not have come to pass had it not been for a dinner I arranged between our wonderful publisher, Myles Thompson, his darling wife, Lee, and my dear friend, Joyce Storey. I had a sudden bolt of inspiration that told me these friends of mine should meet and get to know each other. We had such a fabulous evening at West End Café, laughing and talking, that we didn't want it to end. So we didn't let it end! We moved to the Eastern Standard bar for a nightcap! As I predicted, everyone assembled became fast friends, and after my ninetieth birthday celebration, Myles developed the idea of this passion project. With the right outlook and a passion for connecting friends, life can be so much fun!

Networking celebrates human relationships, shared experiences, and the unexpected thrill of seeing those connections blossom. Whether casually introducing people who go on to form lasting friendships or providing opportunities for others to engage with the arts and culture, networking creates community and nurtures creativity.

In literature, we find countless examples of these introductions leading to life-changing outcomes. Consider Jane Austen's *Pride and Prejudice,* where Elizabeth Bennet and Mr. Darcy are brought together through chance meetings and mutual acquaintances. The two protagonists might never have overcome their initial misunderstandings and prejudices without those subtle connections. Austen's works frequently highlight how pivotal introductions and social circles are in developing relationships, romantic or otherwise.

In F. Scott Fitzgerald's *The Great Gatsby,* we see how Gatsby's lavish parties are social events and networking hubs where art, music, and culture converge, and new friendships are formed. While the novel critiques the excesses of the Jazz Age, it also captures the energy and excitement of such gatherings, where creative minds and influencers mingle, and lifelong connections are often forged.

Today, of course, we have a different kind of influencer: YouTubers, TikTokers and other social media influencers are often invited to restaurant openings, theater performances, brand launches, or any event people want to publicize. "Word of mouth" is still the best endorsement for a good product, even if (and sometimes especially if) that word of mouth is virtual.

Another joyous aspect of networking is its potential to support important causes through events such as fundraisers and galas. These sometimes-glamorous affairs serve as a platform to connect like-minded people who are passionate about a common goal. Imagine a charity auction at a gallery—guests mingling over champagne, bidding on artwork to support a local arts initiative. It's not just about philanthropy; it's about the *thrill* of seeing people engage through their shared commitment to the arts while also contributing to the greater good. Such events create a positive impact as people form personal connections and discover ways to work together toward a cause they care about.

I had the pleasure of meeting Cheryl Black and Kevin Simmons shortly after they moved to Winston-Salem from San Francisco. Of course, I gave them my card. They were a lovely couple and very interesting. Cheryl had recently sold her tech company in Silicon Valley, and Kevin was renovating one of our city's oldest mansions to restore it to its former glory. Unfortunately, they only stayed in Winston-Salem for a few years before moving to Connecticut, where they happily renovated another beautiful home. However, the mark they left on our city in the short time they were here lives on in our memories and in the spectacular renovations they made to that historic mansion. The very same mansion is now owned by a lovely woman named Amy Taylor North, who rents it out as "The Mansion on Main" for special events and short-term rentals. She generously donated it as the space we would use for my ninetieth birthday celebration, where we had a beautiful reception and dinner.

When I met them, I knew Cheryl and Kevin were special people who would be excellent additions to our community. So, I invited them to be my guests at my table for the Magnolia Ball (I always find fresh, exciting people to invite to that event!). I predicted that they would be a great addition to my table of guests, and I was right. They sat beside my dear friend Howell Binkley and his wife, Joyce. The four of them got along famously, and before the night was over, Cheryl and Kevin showed us photos of their incredible sanctuary in Ecuador, and they even invited the Binkleys to visit! Such is the type of magic that happens when you bring like-minded people together. It is profoundly rewarding.

The best part of networking is the sense of community it breeds. Meeting new people and watching those introductions turn into valued relationships creates a network of friends and colleagues that enriches every aspect of one's life. Networking is often spontaneous; its joy lies in the unexpected ways it expands social circles and opens doors.

In the realm of the arts, networking takes on an additional layer of joy. Introducing people to the arts—through a gallery opening, a theater performance, or a museum fundraiser—creates opportunities for cultural enrichment and shared appreciation. Introducing someone to their first opera or contemporary dance performance can open their eyes to a world they had never considered. I was determined to take as many of my students as possible to arts events while teaching. Without exposure, a person might miss the opportunity to tap into passions they never even knew they had!

Howell Binkley (whom I have remembered so fondly throughout this book) was one of those people. I taught him tenth-grade English at Atkins High School during the first year of integration. He was a friendly person who got along with everyone. He was white, and his first friend at Atkins was a black student. As an adult, Howell became a world-renowned theatrical lighting designer. Among his many accomplishments and accolades, he sculpted light for fifty-two Broadway shows (though he started his career in rock n roll), received nine Tony Award nominations, and won two (for *Jersey Boys* and *Hamilton*). He also received two British Olivier Awards (for *Kiss of the Spider Woman* and *Hamilton*), with two NAACP Awards (for *Memphis* and *Ain't Too Proud*) and a multitude of other awards and honors.

Lindsay Jones was another Reynolds graduate. He attended UNCSA-Drama and is now a noted composer and sound designer who is especially proud of his work will all of Shakespeare's plays, He received a Tony nomination for *Slave Play.*

Howell liked language. He liked words. He was intrigued by what you can do with words. When I offered to take students to an opera or a performance, he'd be the first to volunteer to attend. Howell was one of the taller students, and, in my mind's eye, I can still see that long arm shooting up to volunteer! When he designed the lighting for *The Tempest,* he called me. "Mrs. Dunning, you've got to get up here. I'm at the Shakespeare Theatre, and we're doing *The Tempest*."

I said, "Oh my word!"

Then he said, "Do you remember the first time I saw *The Tempest*?"

"No," I replied.

"You took me!" He said it was at Wake Forest, when the theater was on the library's top floor. "And you took a whole bunch of us," he enthusiastically reminded me. Of course, once he recounted it, I remembered.

Later, Howell worked on *Whistle Down the Wind,* the Andrew Lloyd Webber show that didn't make it to Broadway. Howell lovingly called it *Whistle Down the Drain*! I remember sitting next to Michael Kahn, the artistic director of the Shakespeare Theatre Company, on opening night. Directly in front of me were two Secret Service agents—because right in front of them were President George H. W. Bush and his wife Barbara, along with White House chief of staff James Baker and his wife. Directly across the aisle were Andrew Lloyd Webber and his spouse. I'm never good at recognizing celebrities (there are so many I don't know) but I definitely recognized these people!

Howell knew so many interesting people, famous or otherwise. He introduced me to Tony Award-winning actor, Ben Vereen, with whom he had worked. They happened to run into each other when we were at church at Marble Collegiate in New York.

Liza Minelli loved Howell! He did a show with her called *Minelli on Minelli.* She called him up one night and insisted he join her for dinner along with journalist Katie Couric and Liz Smith, "The Grand Dame of Dish." Howell was terrified to join such a prestigious group, but of course he went and had a wonderful evening, though he told me he asked the bartender never to allow his glass to be empty! When Liza signed Howell's show poster, she wrote, "To my darling Bink. I love you. Liza." Howell was charming and disarming and was adored by many.

Oscar, BAFTA, Emmy and two-time Tony award-winning costume designer Paul Tazewell, a School of the Arts grad (with an MFA from NYU), did many shows with Howell. On opening night of *Hamilton* he wrote, "Congrats on your beautiful lighting design! It is truly breathtaking. It is also always very comforting to be working in the same room with you. Until the next...xxxo Paul."

As fate would have it, there were not a lot of "nexts" for Howell, but he lived a big life while he was with us.

My husband Ellis and Howell's father, John Binkley Jr,. traveled in the same circles because of their military connection. John was also a veteran. We would sometimes see him and his wife Louise socially. They were lovely people. Ellis and John would talk about their eldest son, John III, who had a prolific career in the military, retiring as a Colonel. Louise and I would discuss Howell's latest creative endeavors. Howell traveled a lot throughout his career and would always look me up when he was home visiting his parents to tell me of his latest projects.

In her later years, Howell's mother Louise was in a nursing home outside of town. He would invite me to drive out and visit her with him. My presence made the visits easier for him, and I was happy to join.

I attended about forty of Howell's Broadway openings. He would call and invite me, and I'd jump on a plane to New York to attend. The first performance I went to was his Broadway debut, *Kiss of the Spider Woman* starring Chita Rivera (another big fan of Howell's). It was very exciting and beautifully lit. In a tribute at the time of his passing, Chita recalled how amazed she was by Howell's ability to turn her into a spider, complete with intricate web—all using only light. Howell was nominated for his first Tony Award, received a British Olivier Award and a Canadian Dora Award for that design.

Howell always credited his high school English teacher with helping him get into the arts. He said he wouldn't have been exposed to any of it had it not been for all of our field trips. He loved high art. He also swore he would never have made it through high school English without the extra credit he received for those same field trips!

In Charles Dickens's *Great Expectations,* when Pip is introduced to the world of London society, he meets various people who influence his life, shaping his understanding of the world and his place in it. These positive and negative connections teach him valuable life lessons, highlighting how the people we meet along the way shape our journeys. Howell Binkley had an exciting and eclectic journey, shaped by many fascinating people. Indeed, we can *all* undertake such a fascinating journey if we remember the value of community.

At its heart, networking is a joyful process because it's fundamentally about community—about connecting, introducing, and celebrating each other's talents, passions, and potential. From the simple act of introducing two future friends to orchestrating a grand gala that brings people together to support the arts, the joy of networking lies in its ability to create lasting bonds and shared experiences. Through these introductions, we build professional and personal communities that support and inspire us for years.

Don't be shy about pursuing their acquaintance the next time you meet someone you think is interesting. You never know where that introduction may lead. My life has been mightily enriched by the people I've collected and introduced along the way.

Once, when I was in New York at a book signing, I saw a woman across the room. She looked very artistic and had a flair for dressing that made her stand out. I shook her hand, saying, "You look interesting. I just had to meet you!" which was true. The expression on her face was priceless! She was thrilled to have been picked out of the crowd by a stranger, and we proceeded to have the most engaging conversation about life, art, and her connection to the author of the book we were having signed.

I have had many of these types of encounters with people at the most unexpected times. These fortuitous connections speak to our interconnectivity as humans and how the stars and planets somehow align to allow two people in the same place at the exact moment to share an intersection on their respective journeys. Sometimes, these connections grow into friendships that last a lifetime. Other times, they provide lively fellowship for a passing moment. Either way, they are joyous experiences.

I met my good friend, Joyce Storey because of my connection with Howell Binkley. Howell had told me about this woman he'd met at the Union Square Theater in New York while he was working on a delightful show called *Bat Boy: The Musical.*

I said, "Why don't you ask her out?"

"Oh no, she's out of my league!" was his instant reply.

And that appeared to be the end of it.

Joyce was also in theater, and their paths continued to intersect. She worked on the first national tour of his show, *Kiss of the Spider Woman,* but again they never met. She then worked at Manhattan Ensemble Theater in SoHo where Howell did several shows including

Golda's Balcony, which eventually moved to Broadway. Joyce also wrote a magazine column, *Joyce of the Theatre,* and she interviewed Howell several times when he had shows on Broadway or London's West End.

Eventually, he convinced her to create and assist him with his new company, Bentley Productions. I thought they'd never get together romantically! Finally, Joyce left to pursue other creative endeavors. As fate would have it, she ran into Howell in London when she was shooting a movie outside the Piccadilly Theatre. He happened to be inside teching *Avenue Q*!

His first words to her were, "Guess what? I'm IRS compliant and I just got nominated for a Tony Award!"

How she laughed! The nomination news (for *Jersey Boys*) took a backseat to his IRS victory!

Eventually, the day came. I had flown to New York and Joyce and I attended an opening night reception at the West Bank Cafe on 42nd Street. We had the most wonderful evening together and, wanting to get to know this mystery woman, I asked her all sorts of questions about herself.

We came back to Howell's apartment in Harlem and when I got him alone, I said, "Howell Binkley, don't screw this up!"

He took my advice, and they were married at their beautiful beach house in Emerald Isle, North Carolina, shortly thereafter. They have been "chosen family" ever since.

I have been told I could talk to the wall, and I suppose I could! I know more people than an average person might have in their sphere, mainly because I've taught almost everyone in my town! When I was teaching, I had extraordinary students. One after another walked into my classroom and amazed me. Many have become friends over the years. I learned so much from them. People perceive teachers as imparting wisdom to their students, but the road runs both ways. Students have the most incredible insights. They are warm, wonderful people who are excited about life and possibility. When you tap into that excitement, creativity and innovation abound.

It has become a joke among my friends that I know at least one person everywhere I go. Mariedith Appanaitis, my powerhouse friend from the Piedmont Opera, made a button for me that says: "Yes, I am Phyllis Dunning!"

I encourage anyone to instigate an exchange with another person who appears interesting to them. What do you have to lose? You never know who is sitting on the bus beside you (like my future husband!), next to you at a café, or standing in line at the grocery store. Life is all about human interaction. It's one of the most important, rewarding parts of our humanity. I have met many incredible people in my life and my travels. I have had many extraordinary friends. I am grateful for every single one.

I understand that approaching new people can be a more daunting task for some, but the rewards are potentially priceless! Think of all the pleasurable interactions some people miss because they have never introduced themselves. They've robbed themselves of the opportunity for rich conversation. Why not ask someone, "What brought you here today?" and see where the conversation leads. You might find that you have shared interests.

If you are shy or find it difficult to navigate the world of social events, it can feel overwhelming, but with a few strategies, it can become more manageable and even enjoyable. There are ways to approach social situations with confidence, like conversing with one or two people or staying for a specific amount of time.

My friend Veda Storey has seven delightful, now grown, children. They have a code among them for attending social events. When they are ready to leave, someone simply says, "Shall we?"

Before they leave home, they ask, "What time are we 'shall we-ing'?"

They prepare their exit before leaving home and then go with the flow. The "Shall we?" hour is adjusted if they are having a good time.

If I could, I would connect every lonely person with another human being. Spending time with people, getting to know them, learning from them, laughing with them, having stimulating conversations, and sharing the best of life make one's journey fulfilled and enriched.

I encourage anyone to put themselves out there and see where it goes. You don't always have to be the one initiating conversation. Maybe you'll get lucky and end up sitting beside someone like me and I guarantee, you'll be out of the gate in no time! Just show up and see where that takes you. If you're open to engaging when someone approaches you, the conversation could lead anywhere. You can also bring a friend to an event. If nothing else, you'll have a good time visiting with one another.

I have been fortunate in my life and career to meet extraordinary people. Each has been a unique gem among the riches of friends and acquaintances I have made. Friendship is one of the most enriching elements of life and fills your cup in profound ways that benefit your emotional, mental, and even physical well-being.

Friends embody so many virtues that define meaningful and lasting relationships. They stand by you through good times and bad, offering consistent support without wavering in their commitment. They understand you in ways that others might not. This mutual understanding, cultivated over time, leads to a deep sense of validation and acceptance. Friends often reflect our values, helping us understand ourselves better. They accept us for who we are without judgment. This unconditional acceptance is life-affirming, helping us feel valued and loved for our true selves.

Friends provide a safe space to share your joys, fears, and challenges. Knowing they won't betray your confidence, you can trust them with your thoughts, secrets, and vulnerabilities. A loyal friend gives you a sense of trust and security that strengthens your emotional resilience. Knowing someone has your back no matter what can fill your life with confidence and reduce anxiety.

Good friends understand and share your feelings, showing genuine concern for your experiences and offering comfort in times of need. They respect your boundaries, opinions, and individuality. They value who you are without trying to change or control you. They offer genuine support and provide constructive feedback when necessary, even if it might be uncomfortable. They value truth in the relationship. Whether celebrating success or dealing with failure, a good friend is there to encourage you, lift your spirits, and help you grow. Their presence during difficult times offers comfort and helps lighten emotional burdens. Knowing that you have someone who truly cares and listens replenishes your emotional reserves, making life's difficulties more bearable.

True friends encourage you to grow and evolve. They challenge you to be your best self and offer honest feedback, advice, and motivation when needed. Their belief in your potential can inspire you to pursue goals and dreams you might have doubted on your own.

They enhance happiness by sharing moments of joy and laughter. Whether reminiscing about good times or simply sharing a funny moment, spending time with friends fills your cup with lightheartedness and positive energy. Friends create shared experiences through travel, hobbies, or meaningful conversations, deepening connections and creating cherished memories that last a lifetime.

Friends come in all shapes, sizes, and ages. I have many friends my age but also many who are much younger. One vibrant youthful soul in my circle is Jenna Anderson, who overcame great odds to study at UNCSA. After graduating, she opened her own shop, Jenna Sais Quoi, creating custom apparel, costumes, dancewear and limited edition collections. Such a clever name, such a clever girl!

Surrounding yourself with younger people as you age can be incredibly revitalizing and essential for overall well-being. The younger generation brings new perspectives, energy, and enthusiasm that can be inspiring and refreshing. As we age, their openness to new ideas and evolving social trends can challenge us to stay curious and engaged with the world. They encourage us to adopt healthier habits, embrace technology, and maintain a sense of relevance in a rapidly changing world.

By bridging generational gaps, people exchange wisdom and new ideas, adding a sense of purpose and connection to both generations. This dynamic can reduce feelings of isolation, improve one's mental health, and uplift daily life, nurturing both body and mind. Young people are vibrant and full of life. I challenge everyone "of an age" to befriend a younger person. Your life will be better for knowing them.

This was my experience when I met Katie Hall Nicolas at the Opening Convocation of Salem College in 2010. She was a student, and I served on the school's board of visitors. I was the first alumna friend she had met. We instantly became fast friends despite our fifty-two-year age gap! I brought her to her first symphony concert, and we have attended innumerable arts events since then. Katie is a presence and a force. The mayor of Winston-Salem adores her. When Katie was a student at Salem, she interned in the mayor's office.

She walked into the mayor's office and said, "I want to meet you."

She made an appointment, went for the brass ring, and got what she wanted.

When I was in the hospital for six days, who came to the hospital room every morning, brought her computer, and worked from that room every day, morning to night? Katie. She is incredible. She planned a fantastic event for my ninetieth birthday. She is very clever and light years ahead of many of her contemporaries. She and her wonderful French husband, Jonathan, have started a family, recently welcoming their first child, Maxence into the world. They live in the house directly behind me and drop by to see me regularly. I am so blessed to have them in my life, all because I introduced myself to a student and Salem Sister.

Sadly, I have lost several dear friends and family members over time. We all do as we age. It is part of the cycle of life. Though it is tough to lose a loved one, and our hearts are heavy with grief, I give thanks for each encounter we shared on our journey together. My life has forever changed because I have known them. Isn't it wonderful that I had them for as long as I did?

Márta Blades was a dear, dear person. She was an artist with a discerning eye. Her condo was in Tar Branch Towers, above a restaurant and bar called the Meridian. I go there on Wednesday evenings for happy hour. There, I see friends, drink wine, engage in interesting conversation, and often meet new people.

Márta was one of those people. She had moved to Winston-Salem from Indianapolis and had such a remarkable history. She wrote a book for her grandchildren so they would know where they came from: *Leaves from an Unexpected Life: A Refugee's Journey.*

Márta was born in Transylvania and attended a girls' school in Budapest. When the Russians and the war came, her family fled to Germany. Her family was very prominent in Hungary, and they had some relationships with royalty. The country had famous horses; the people there didn't want the Russians to take the horses because they knew they would probably kill them for food. Márta's family covertly escaped the country after they moved the horses. She attended a girls' school in Germany and then came to the United States on a scholarship to a school in Indiana.

At college, she met a young man named William Blades. She married him and stayed in the United States. They had two daughters and a son: Michelle lives in Indianapolis; their son lives in Key West, Florida; and Marija lives in Winston-Salem.

Marija and her husband Brian, an attorney, wanted Márta to move here and live near them. They said, "Mother, the medical facilities and the weather are good. It's a lovely city." They convinced her to move. They had a large condo, and a smaller one was available next to theirs. They also had nearby property in Stokes County, some room in the house, and a guest house. So, Márta left her dear friends and art gallery and moved here.

Ramelle and Michael Pulitzer lived in Winston-Salem then, and Ramelle owned an art gallery, where Márta exhibited. I bought the first work Márta sold in Winston-Salem. I couldn't buy a big one, so I bought a smaller painting. It is hanging in my kitchen.

She was such an exciting person. She lived alone and didn't drive. I'd attend many events and say, "I'm going to a concert at the School of the Arts. Would you like to join me?"

And she would say, "I'd love to!"

"Great, I'll pick you up," I'd reply.

She would mention a movie she was looking forward to seeing, and I'd say, "Which day can you go? I'll pick you up." We attended plays, concerts, shows, and movies. In a short time, she became a dear friend. Márta shared my love of books.

Márta, too, wrote a book about her life. Her book ends with the following passage:

> Baptized by my friend Katie, "The Wonderful Women's Wednesday Wine Club" happens every Wednesday at the Meridian

> Restaurant in Winston-Salem. The membership changes from one Wednesday to the next, but chances are one will find Winston-Salem's Grand Dame, Miss Phyllis, there. She's the beloved English teacher whose students, now grown-up and some quite famous, stop by just to see her, along with many neighbors and visitors from all over. We're grateful that she keeps us up to date on the fantastic schedule of events at the UNCSA, University of North Carolina School of the Arts. Be it theater, dance, or music, it's always superb. Knowing more about Winston-Salem than most, she shares its stories with joy.

Some people find it more difficult to approach others than I do. It saddens me to think of all the pleasurable interactions they miss because they have never given themselves the opportunity for life-changing conversations. I encourage anyone to instigate an exchange with another person who appears interesting to them. What do you have to lose? You never know who is sitting on the bus beside you (like my future husband!), next to you at a café, or standing in line at the grocery store. Life is all about human interaction. It's one of the most important, rewarding parts of our humanity. I have met many extraordinary people in my life and my travels. I have had many extraordinary friends. I am grateful for every single one.

My life has been a testament to the deep value of friends and the many connections we can nurture. Companionship and connection are essential to human happiness. Why not connect with someone today? Have a coffee, go to the park. *Carpe diem!*

LESSON 17

PURSUIT OF EXCELLENCE

Knowledge without practice is useless. Practice without knowledge is dangerous.

—Confucius

Many of my students went into the arts and became writers, composers, actors, directors, and designers. The sheer number of students for whom this is true is mind-boggling. Winston-Salem has fantastic talent, and I was fortunate enough to teach many talented people. On the surface, it seems to be a disproportionate number—more than usual—but I believe the reason lies in our rich heritage.

The Moravians, known for their emphasis on education, community, and deeply rooted spirituality, settled in this region in the mid-eighteenth century. Their church is a Protestant denomination that originated in the early fifteenth century in the Czech Republic.

In the 1750s, seeking a place to practice their faith and establish a free communal society, the Moravians purchased a large tract of land in North Carolina. They named it "The Wachovia Tract," after the Wachau Valley in Austria, where the church had historical ties. The Moravians then built their first settlement in Wachovia, called Bethabara, in 1753. The settlers worked to create a self-sustaining community that could support religious, economic, and educational life. Bethabara became an early hub for trade, attracting Native Americans and other European settlers. The Moravians only saw it as a *temporary* location, however, and they sought a more central location to build and establish their main settlement.

In 1766, they founded Salem, intended to be the heart of their community and a spiritual center. The town was meticulously planned to emphasize communal values and separate residential and workshop areas. Salem became a thriving town known for its trades, crafts, and educational institutions. The Moravians set up businesses including pottery, blacksmithing, and tailoring, and Salem quickly became an economic center in the area. They also built a church in the center of Salem (Home Moravian Church), which became the focal point of their spiritual lives. Salem was governed by church elders, who ensured that the community adhered to the Moravian values of simplicity, hard work, and faith.

By the nineteenth century, Salem's influence expanded as it engaged with neighboring communities. In 1849, the nearby town of Winston was established as the county seat of the newly formed Forsyth County. Named after Revolutionary War hero Joseph Winston, the town began as a small settlement near Salem's more extensive, well-established Moravian community. Winston rapidly grew in the late nineteenth century, transforming into a booming industrial hub primarily driven by the tobacco and textile industries.

The Reynolds family was one of the most influential industrial families in Winston's history. Richard Joshua (R. J.) Reynolds, a Virginia native, established the R.J. Reynolds Tobacco Company in Winston in 1875. His company quickly became one of the largest tobacco producers in the United States, with products like Camel cigarettes fueling the growth of both the company and the town. R. J. Reynolds's business success attracted workers and spurred economic activity, helping turn Winston into a prosperous industrial center.

The Hanes family was another major contributor to Winston's industrial development. Brothers John Wesley Hanes and Pleasant Henderson Hanes established textile and hosiery companies that would later grow into the globally recognized Hanesbrands. The Hanes businesses became essential to Winston's economy, creating employment opportunities and establishing the city as a center for textiles.

In 1913, Winston merged with Salem to form Winston-Salem, blending the industrial might of Winston with Salem's cultural heritage. The legacies of the Reynolds and Hanes families continue to shape the city, whose skyline, economy, and philanthropic landscape bear the marks of these pioneering industrialists.

While Winston contributed its industrial might, Salem preserved its Moravian heritage and distinct architecture, which is still visible in the historic Old Salem area. The legacy of the Moravian settlers is evident throughout Winston-Salem. The Old Salem Museums & Gardens preserve many original structures, offering a glimpse into eighteenth-century Moravian life. The Moravian traditions, including distinctive holiday celebrations, music, and culinary customs, remain integral to the city's cultural fabric. Through their commitment to faith, community, and education, the Moravian settlers profoundly shaped Winston-Salem, creating a unique blend of heritage and modernity that continues to define the city.

Music and education are of central importance in the Moravian culture. The Moravians not only educated males, but they also had a strong tradition of educating females. Schooling and education have always been paramount for all Moravians. They also had a tradition of fine craftsmanship, producing many great potters, gunmakers, and silversmiths. Everybody in the Moravian community had a craft and trade. When industrial families like the Reynolds, the Grays, the Hanes, and the Stocktons created wealth and introduced it to the cultural Moravian mix, it was a powerful combination.

In 1949, Winston-Salem became home to the first arts council in the United States, setting a model for arts support and community engagement. Founded as the Arts Council of Winston-Salem and Forsyth County, the organization provided consistent funding, coordination, and support for various arts initiatives within the community. This innovative approach brought together different art forms, including visual arts, theater, dance, and music, under one umbrella, fostering collaboration and creating a vibrant cultural ecosystem.

The council's efforts helped establish Winston-Salem as a prominent center for the arts in the Southeast and inspired the creation of similar organizations across the nation. Today, the Arts Council supports local artists and cultural programs, solidifying Winston-Salem's reputation as the "City of Arts and Innovation." My dear friend Katie Hall Nicolas was an integral to the Council for several years.

A city of arts, higher education, and industrial innovation makes a potent breeding ground for future generations of talent and excellence. With such an impressive legacy, it's no wonder that I had so many superstars in my classes. As I've said, my students were some of my best teachers. I learned so much from them. They were (and continue to be) terrific people.

Michael Wilson, who became a Broadway director, was my student in his senior year at Reynolds High School. Among his many accomplishments, Michael directed the Tony Award-winning Broadway revival of Horton Foote's *A Trip to Bountiful* (starring Cicely Tyson, Cuba Gooding Jr., Vanessa Williams, and Condola Rashad). He also directed the subsequent Emmy Award-winning film adaptation. On Broadway, he directed the Tony-nominated revival of Gore Vidal's *The Best Man* (starring James Earl Jones, Angela Lansbury, Candice Bergen, John Larroquette, Eric McCormack, John Stamos, Kristin Davis, and Michael McKean); the Tony-nominated *Dividing the Estate* (starring Elizabeth Ashley and Gerald McRaney); and *Enchanted April* (starring Jayne Atkinson and Molly Ringwald).

Michael was our student body president in his final year of high school. He was a delightful student. He was in the same class as Stuart Scott, who became a sportscaster and anchor on ESPN, including on SportsCenter, covering both the NBA and NFL. Sadly, Stuart died young of cancer. In my class, Stuart sat in front, and Michael sat behind him. Joe Shugart, who later was Michael's roommate at Chapel Hill, sat next to Stuart. Shugart is a well-known Moravian name in Winston-Salem, and Joe is now a film editor in Los Angeles. He has worked on many films and series, including *Cyborg, Jacob's Ladder, Starting Over, Swamp People,* and *Life Below Zero.*

What an impressive class that was! Three superstars were sitting with each other, boom-boom-boom! And there were many others. As I continue to say (because it is true and I feel so fortunate), I had great students. Winston-Salem was a perfect place for them to grow up and become exposed to the arts and all things possible within that field. When young people see others succeed before them, they think, *I can do that!* And they do.

Michael was an avid drama lover. He received the University of North Carolina at Chapel Hill's Morehead-Cain Scholarship (we locals usually just call it "The Morehead"). The foundation aims to identify, invest in, and empower a community of dynamic, purpose-driven leaders. Created by John Motley Morehead III in 1951, the scholarship was inspired by the Rhodes Scholarship at Oxford University and meant to attract the brightest and best to Chapel Hill. For a high school senior fortunate enough to receive a Morehead scholarship, it means full tuition for four years, including a summer internship in the private or corporate sector and travel abroad (as well as many other ancillary cultural and networking opportunities). It's a big deal.

I taught several students who received a Morehead, as well as many who were nominated but did not receive it. I used to ask those nominated students: "Do you realize what an elite group you are now a part of?" I would tell them about some people who preceded them who did not attain the scholarship, and the list was *impressive.* Even to be nominated for a Morehead is an honor that indicates how outstanding you are.

Many "Moreheads" have impressive careers in law, medicine, and business. However, few pursue careers in the arts. I was fortunate to teach several who did.

The Morehead is not only about academics. It is heavily invested in leadership. Recipients must be well-rounded. It is a prerequisite that a viable candidate must participate in a sport. Many students who prefer the arts don't happen to play a sport, but Michael was not only academically and artistically brilliant, he also excelled in fencing.

Another Morehead scholar who was a student of mine, Robbie Bach, was named an Academic All-American on the Tar Heels varsity tennis team at the University of North Carolina at Chapel Hill. He graduated with the highest honors in economics and would later become the president of Microsoft's entertainment and devices division, which was responsible for the Xbox, Xbox 360, Zune, Games for Windows, Windows Phone, and the Microsoft TV platform. He retired after twenty-two years working for Microsoft. He then wrote a novel, *The Wilkes Insurrection: A Contemporary Thriller.* I, of course, have a copy.

Another talented student, Jess Perry, moved to San Francisco after earning a bachelor's degree in voice performance from UNC-Chapel Hill and a master's in operatic performance from Boston Conservatory at Berklee. For years, he sang with the San Francisco Opera chorus. He then moved into management, becoming a senior budget manager. In high school, Jess was a swimmer.

Many of my students aspired to a tradition of excellence. They saw others succeed, and they followed in their footsteps. And it did not occur to them that they couldn't do it. Being raised in a culture that values the pursuit of excellence is not just a powerful motivator; it is a path to success.

I kept in touch with Michael because I always went to all the local arts events, and of course, he did as well. At Chapel Hill, he worked with the PlayMakers, the university's big theater. I would attend his shows. I also attended their humanities series when he returned, at the invitation of the university, to be on the panel. And I have proudly attended many of his incredible shows in New York.

When Michael was Associate Director at the Alley Theater in Houston, Texas, my ninety-year-old friend Dr. Gib Yokley asked me to accompany him to Houston so he could attend his dental school class reunion. His wife had passed away, and he was unable to make the trip alone. Michael was directing *Long Day's Journey Into Night* starring Ellen Burstyn and was thrilled to find out that I would be in Houston and attending his show. Not only did Michael get me tickets, he arranged for me to go to the Houston Ballet, Houston Symphony, Houston Opera and also introduced me to the famous playwright Horton Foote and Horton's daughter Hallie. Wow! Just wow!

Gib thought it was so funny. He said, "I knew *I* was going to have a good time at my reunion, but hell, I didn't know *you* were going to have more fun than I did!"

How we laughed!

When I taught at Reynolds, I had five eleventh-grade classes of academically gifted students. I learned from them, and I repeat it because I mean it!

Karen Wong, one of my students, became the director of the New Museum of Contemporary Art in New York City and has held several other positions there. She co-founded the first museum-born incubator for art, design, and technology and is an adjunct assistant professor at Columbia Graduate School of Architecture, Planning and Preservation. She lectures on museum innovation and emergent culture. She is a brilliant woman, and she was brilliant as a student.

One of my very interesting and exceedingly bright students was Hans Salzwedel. He came from a beautiful Moravian family. His father James was the Minister of Music at Home Moravian Church and started the Hussite Bell Ringers during his ministry. He and his wife, Sarah, had three sons, Hans, Erik and Karl. I didn't teach Erik because he went to School of the Arts for high school (he's a musician), but I did teach Hans and Jonathan. Jonathan and Hans were so different. Jonathan was quiet and did everything by the book. Hans was a *real* rebel.

This may surprise other educators, but I *loved* the rebels. They were just living their best lives. And Hans was a character! Getting him to turn in his work was a herculean task!

I remember at one time saying, "Hans Salzwedel, you are going to turn in that paper if I have to come and sit on your family's doorstep until I get it!"

Eventually, he turned it in. He was very smart and very negligent about his work.

After high school he went to UNC Greensboro, then Carolina. He had all sorts of majors but finally settled on Philosophy. Once he got his degree, he decided he wanted to become a doctor. He went to NC State for all of the science courses he needed to apply for medical school. He got his medical degree and he was an excellent psychiatrist in California for many years until he retired. He treated many patients with a wide array of problems. Some of his patients had been in prison.

One day after school, when Hans was in college, my students had all gone and I was still working. Along came this bicycle and Hans appeared at my doorway. He had ridden his bike on the landing and down the hall to our classroom.

He announced, "I've come by to tell you what I'm majoring in. I was going to study [such and such]. Then I decided, no, I'd rather do..."

He'd thought about history and English and all sorts of other subjects but then decided he was just going to be a philosophy major. He was just so smart! He would have succeeded at anything.

That day I remember one of the things I said, "Oh Hans, I bet you've come back to check on your artwork."

He said, "What artwork?"

I said, "I so regret to have to tell you that I had to erase and wash away all of the artwork on your desk, but your artwork on the ceiling has not been touched."

He said, "You knew I did that…?"

I said, "Hans, of course I knew. I'm not blind."

And he said, "But you never said anything."

And I said, "Would it have changed anything?"

He laughed! When he was my student, he would make spit balls with paper, then he would shoot them at the ceiling—so, there they still were. They had dried and were stuck to the ceiling semi-permanently. I couldn't reach them to get them off, and as a busy teacher, I felt I had bigger fish to fry.

Regarding all of the things he had drawn and written and etched into his desk, I had to say, "I'm sorry, but that's all gone."

These kids… Funny. Brilliant. Sometimes, especially boys don't apply themselves initially and then they are inspired by something they're interested in and they just fly.

I used to say to my classes, "Don't ever say you're bored, because if you don't like what's happening, you have a mind and an imagination: follow that. There is no reason (no excuse *ever*) to be bored. Ever. Just let your brain and your imagination take you on a trip."

I suspected that, a lot of times, they were letting their imaginations take them on trips during class. Don't you think that's true? There is no excuse in this life to sit there and be bored.

Watching my former students blossom into adults and seeing where their paths took them is very gratifying. When Ben Folds was my student, I had no idea he would become the star he is now, but I enjoyed his creativity and fresh perspective on the world. He played music standing up and bouncing his leg (he still does!). He built his audience in Nashville, then got an agent, and the rest (as they say) is history. His book is always on my coffee table, and I think of him often.

I'm also proud of the many other stars and bright students that came out of my classroom. Wilton Barnhardt, one of my favorite people, was among them. He loves great food and wine: he's a consummate gourmand. He has written five novels (*Emma Who Saved My Life; Gospel; Show World; Lookaway, Lookaway;* and *Western Alliances*) and has traveled the world. Interestingly, Wilton doesn't fly, so he has taken ships, trains, buses, and automobiles to various exotic destinations.

I once traveled with Wilton and my friend Betty Greg on a crossing of the *Queen Elizabeth 2*. It took about five days, and we spent three weeks in France and Spain. It was fabulous because Wilton is the best tour guide. He's a seasoned traveler and smart as a whip. The last time he visited Russia, he took along Amor Towles's historical fiction novel *A Gentleman in Moscow*. He stayed at the Hotel Metropol: the grand hotel that is the setting for the novel. When he left the hotel, he gave his copy of the book to the hotel staff. He's a remarkable individual.

His book, *Gospel,* takes place across Europe and the Middle East. Any location that Wilton writes about, he has visited. One of my favorite books of his, *Gospel* is about the discovery of another gospel, and in the narrative many people are trying to get their hands on it for various reasons. Every other chapter is an excerpt from the imaginary gospel; the chapters are people trying to use, destroy, or protect it. There are *lots* of footnotes. Initially, I thought, "Well, maybe I will skip the gospel bits and just read the story." But I read everything, including the footnotes, because the story drew me in completely.

I know two people who are basically walking encyclopedias. One was Jack Felts, a local doctor. He and his wife Kitty were friends of mine who have both since passed. Wilton is the *same* type of encyclopedic person—a voracious reader who remembers everything he's ever read, heard, or seen.

I called him William in high school because he signed William on his papers, but his classmates who had been with him since elementary school called him Billy. After he had written his first book, he started using his middle name, Wilton, because there were other writers named William Barnhardt. So, now, a lot of times, I call him Billy William Wilton!

"Billy William Wilton, where are you now?!"

He and Joyce Carter were best buds in school. They were both clever and creative. They would write skits, monologues, and dialogues, and then Wilton could sit at the piano and play music to accompany the skits. They were hilarious! Wilton is a wordsmith: *so* talented. Both of them had such a wild sense of humor. Joyce could do imitations of all the faculty members, including *moi.*

Her mother and I graduated in the same high school class, and her father, Doug Carter, was the arts director for the school system. He began and led the summer enrichment program for students in the arts. I knew Joyce and her sister, Sarah, from the time they were born. Joyce was born with spina bifida and was not expected to live to adulthood, yet fortunately she did. Unfortunately, she passed away four or five years ago. She was amazing. She went to Trinity Moravian Church, and every year, she would write things the congregation could perform at different times of year. Both she and Wilton were great wits. And Joyce was a walking book. Talk about an avid reader!

I used to say, "Give Joyce Carter a stack of books and tomato sandwiches made with Duke's Mayonnaise, and you will have sent her to heaven!"

City with Dwellings, an outreach organization that connects people with essential services, was Joyce Carter's primary charity. She constantly worked with people experiencing homelessness. The organization sets up tents and shower trailers, among other services, so people experiencing homelessness can use its facilities. Joyce was passionate about feeding the people who needed to be fed. She would organize and rally to compel people to donate food. She was amazing, and every time I contribute to City with Dwellings, I do so in memory of Joyce.

Howell Binkley (whom I have mentioned lovingly throughout this book) was another exceptional student. I remember receiving information from the Little Theatre in Winston-Salem that they were starting a program called A.C.T.: Acting Classes for Teenagers. Howell was then in the tenth grade, in the first class of white students to come to Atkins.

I told him, "Now, Howell, you ought to go to this A.C.T. program at the Little Theatre. They will teach the participants activities and techniques, and I'm sure there will be some that you can come back and share with the class."

He eagerly said, "Yes, I can do that!"

Of course, I had no idea this would be the beginning of his career in the theater. But I knew it would be an excellent artistic opportunity for Howell and might help my class when he returned and taught them interactive theater exercises.

In that first class of blended students, I had a problem. I had never made seating charts. I said, "Sit where you can be the best student you can be. Some prefer to sit at the front, some like the back, and some prefer to be near the window. So, you choose and that will be your seat."

I can still picture all of the students when they first started—black girls clustered, white girls clustered, black boys clustered, and white boys clustered. They clustered with people they already knew and felt comfortable with. I thought, "Oh my word! I've got to do something about this!" I had never had that issue before, because everybody was the same race. I panicked, thinking: "What will I do to get these students to interact with each other?"

Gradually, they were starting to interact, but I decided to speed up their integration with theater. Howell helped by teaching us all some things he had learned at the Little Theatre. I chose some short one-act plays that would get students in front of the class and acting out parts.

I had inner-city students, students from Ardmore and Country Club neighborhoods, and some from the country (because we had combined the city and county systems just a year or so before that). So, I picked three contrasting plays. One was *The Amen Corner* by James Baldwin, the story of a black female pastor of a storefront Harlem church. Another was *The Education of H*Y*M*A*N K*A*P*L*A*N,* the musical book by Benjamin Bernard Zavin based on Leo Rosten's stories of the fictitious Hyman Kaplan (an immigrant struggling to learn English in a night class in 1920s New York). And the third play was *No Time for Sergeants,* a comedy by Ira Levin (Andy Griffith starred in the film version)—It was the story of a backwoods hillbilly-turned-new-recruit in the Air Force.

I chose those pieces because the language in each play was very different. The students didn't have to memorize their parts; we would just read them.

I had multiple copies, and instead of the students reciting their lines in their seats, I would say: "Come on up to the front of the class so that everyone can hear."

Students would take on different roles, even if they were not exactly the type of person the author had probably imagined for the part. For example, *The Amen Corner* was not just for black students. With *Hyman Kaplan,* it wasn't like we had many New York Jewish students. I was purposely casting against type, which would get the students interacting in new and unusual ways in the front of the classroom. There were a lot of laughs, and I thought getting the students to mix and mingle "onstage" worked very well in terms of breaking down their barriers.. Sometimes, *I* would cast the roles, and sometimes, I would get eager volunteers. Sometimes, I would be the one volunteering *them!*

Once they were all intermingling, some students felt comfortable enough to switch their seats. Seating became a nonissue once the class began to really *gel.* Using drama to get the students to feel comfortable with one another worked exceptionally well, even though they were playing characters that many people at that time would have argued the students were "not suitable for": the transformative power of the arts, in action, once again.

On Broadway, it arguably wasn't until *Hamilton* came along that casting functioned in a similar way with any kind of regularity. I was casting against type in 1970! Now, everybody casts against type. They've seen it done, and they know it can work. They rethink plays, and they stage them in a reimagined way.

I wanted to show my students what was possible. The fair city of Winston-Salem is steeped in traditions that have modeled what is possible for many.

When people believe they can, they can. It's as simple as that.

Always strive for the pursuit of excellence.

LESSON 18

WHAT IS A LIFE WELL LIVED?

Tell me, what is it you plan to do
With your one wild and precious life?
—Mary Oliver, "The Summer Day"

I have given the following questions a lot of thought in my ninety plus years: How does one live their life well? What does a life-well-lived even mean?

A well-lived life is often regarded as imbued with purpose, fulfillment, and positive impact. But what does it *truly* mean to live well? The answer is deeply personal, reflecting your values, beliefs, and aspirations. Ask yourself how you want to live. What is important to you? What do you want to accomplish in your lifetime? Most importantly, how do you find peace, fulfillment, and happiness? I admire so many people who also inspire me and I would like to share a few examples of these inspirational people with you:.

My friend Susan Melville leads a rich and intentional life. She was an excellent English teacher and has had a spectacular career. She is intellectually robust, curious, extraordinarily bright, and has many talents and attributes.

Living purposefully requires aligning our actions, choices, and goals with a meaningful aim. Susan is a lifelong, passionate pursuer of knowledge and information. She and her husband, Charles, have attended over a hundred seminars at Chapel Hill's acclaimed humanities program (an outreach of the university). What an impressive accomplishment! I don't know anyone else who has partaken in that many seminars.

Many friends of mine (and many people whom I do not know personally, but who inspire me nonetheless) are living proof that a well-lived life is not merely about success, wealth, or material gain. Life is about creating meaningful connections, growing continually, and leaving a positive imprint on this earth. It is the pursuit of purpose, personal growth, and compassion.

Purpose can vary greatly. For one person, it might mean raising a family with love and devotion, while for another, it could be creating art that inspires others or building a business that makes a positive social impact. Having a purpose gives a person a sense of direction and adds significance to their actions.

Malala Yousafzai is a globally renowned advocate for girls' education and the youngest-ever Nobel Peace Prize laureate. Despite facing a near-fatal attack by the Taliban at the age of fifteen for championing education in her home country of Pakistan, Malala emerged stronger, dedicating her life to ensuring every girl has access to schooling. Through her organization, the Malala Fund, she works tirelessly to break down barriers to education worldwide. Malala embodies a purposeful life by using her voice to fight against injustice, empowering millions with the courage to stand up for their rights. With her words and dedication, she inspires perseverance: "When the whole world is silent, even one voice becomes powerful."

Malala continues to inspire hope and action globally: "Let us remember: One child, one teacher, one book, and one pen can change the world." Someone who dedicates their life to teaching can find a sense of purpose in nurturing the next generation, shaping young minds, and leaving a lasting impact on society. I certainly hope that I have done that. During my teaching years, I had the most rewarding experiences. Living with purpose doesn't require grand gestures; it can be as simple as making someone's day brighter; one small act at a time. This sense of purpose, big or small, infuses life with meaning and helps us prioritize our actions.

A well-lived life often becomes evident as a result of continual growth and self-improvement. This growth can be intellectual, emotional, or spiritual, enriching a person's life by expanding their perspectives. Continual learning helps us adapt to change, develop resilience, and become the best versions of ourselves. Growth might mean taking on challenges that push us out of our comfort zones, like learning new skills, traveling to unfamiliar places, or developing deeper self-awareness through introspection.

My friend Rebecca Mercer-White in New York City chose to earn her PhD in her early sixties. She *never* considered that she might be too old to pursue higher education. She had a family and a prolific career as a successful opera singer; still, she felt it was time to pivot professionally and expand her knowledge in an area that excited her. She is now an expert in her field, teaching coping strategies to adults with Asperger's syndrome. Despite the challenges of juggling work, family, and studies, she pursued her education, deepened her understanding of the world, and expanded her personal and professional life.

Marie Curie, the first woman to win a Nobel Prize and the only person to win Nobel Prizes in two scientific fields (physics and chemistry), also inspires me. She dedicated her life to scientific discovery. Though she faced significant obstacles as a female scientist in the early twentieth century, Curie's research on radioactivity paved the way for breakthroughs in medicine and nuclear science. Her commitment to learning, perseverance, and intellectual curiosity demonstrates how a well-lived life can mean pursuing knowledge, challenging norms, and advancing humanity.

In a very different field and at another time in history, another inspirational human, Leonardo da Vinci, exemplified a spirit of curiosity and continual growth. Renowned for his contributions as an artist, scientist, and inventor, da Vinci pursued knowledge in every area he could: anatomy, mathematics, engineering, and more. His art and inventions were ahead of their time, and his works, including the *Mona Lisa* and *The Last Supper*, are still revered today. He lived his life relentlessly in pursuit of knowledge and creativity. In the words of the master himself: "As a well spent day brings happy sleep, so life well used brings happy death."

A well-lived life can mean developing one's talents, exploring multiple interests, and leaving a lasting impact on culture and knowledge. People are social creatures, and forming strong bonds with others also contributes to a well-lived life, bringing joy, security, and purpose.

Positive relationships with family, friends, and the community create a support network and bring joy and meaning to the experience of life.

Imagine someone who prioritizes staying connected with their family, checking in regularly with parents, siblings, or old friends. They invest time and energy in nurturing these bonds, which bring warmth and stability to their lives. People might contribute to their community through volunteering or acts of kindness, which gives them a sense of belonging. As I hope I have been able to convince you in this as well as previous chapters of this book, positive connections and community involvement make people feel appreciated and less alone, contributing to their self-fulfillment.

Another essential element of a well-lived life is practicing kindness and compassion. Helping others and being compassionate elevates those who receive kindness and those who give it. When we positively impact others, we derive a sense of satisfaction and joy that cannot be achieved through self-centered pursuits. Small acts of kindness, like offering support to a struggling colleague or comforting a friend in need, are beautiful moments of compassion. These actions, whether grand or small, create ripples of positivity and contribute to a fulfilling life. A compassionate life can leave an enduring legacy of love and kindness, ensuring one's impact resonates well after death.

Living a life of peace and happiness involves adopting values like compassion, simplicity, and purpose. By living intentionally, we steer our actions and choices with awareness rather than simply reacting to circumstances as they unfold. Without intentionality, we risk becoming like leaves blown by the wind—drifting through life at the mercy of external forces, reacting instinctively rather than responding thoughtfully.

My friend Jorge Soccolich, who is from Venezuela, had an uncle who lived in Winston-Salem, and when he was in seventh grade, his parents sent him to live with his uncle in Ardmore during the school year. He lived in Winston-Salem for seventh and eighth grades and returned to Venezuela during the summers. I met him when he was in ninth grade, when the first white students came to Atkins. He was the most diligent student;he wanted to learn and write perfectly. As a young immigrant, he understood the importance of education.

The other students called him George, and they would say to me, "Oh, Mrs. Dunning, George puts us to shame, doesn't he? George works so much harder. We ought to be ashamed of ourselves!"

I simply replied, "I didn't say that; *you* said it. And you are smart enough to know whether or not it's true."

They could see that compared to them, Jorge worked very, very hard.

Two years later, I transferred to Reynolds where I taught juniors, and Jorge was a senior. He was, of course, in the National Honor Society. Academically, he was a marvel. He would often come by my room to say hi, and sometimes, he would stay and chat. When he graduated, he went to the University of Memphis. When he was home for Thanksgiving or Christmas break, he would come by Reynolds to see me. One year, his fourteen-year-old brother was with him, visiting from Venezuela.

I reminded Jorge, "He is the same age you were when I met you. You were in ninth grade, fourteen years old."

Over the years, Jorge and I have kept in touch. He earned his degree in Memphis, then his master's, and then he went to Venezuela to work for a year or two. He then took a job as an engineer in Brownsville, Texas. He married and had two daughters. Now, he has two little grandsons. Jorge periodically visits Winston-Salem and always looks me up. The last time Jorge visited, I had become acquainted with a dermatologist from Venezuela, so Jorge, the dermatologist and I had dinner together. We had a wonderful time. That dermatologist later visited Jorge and his family in Texas. Connections can be so meaningful and so much fun!

When I celebrated my ninetieth birthday, Jorge came to celebrate with me. He's a fine young man who lives intentionally. I always consider him young, even though he's now a grandfather!

For my birthday, he gave me an angel figurine inscribed with the message: "Teachers inspire us to achieve our dreams." Jorge certainly achieved his dreams through hard work and focused attention.

I have received several angel figurines from various students over the years. One depicts an angel holding an apple with the message "Best Teacher Ever." I treasure it.

When we approach life thoughtfully, we develop the ability to pause, reflect, and fully engage with our experiences. We recognize our thoughts, emotions, and actions without judgment and understand how they influence our decisions. We then gain a sense of agency over our lives, aligning our choices with our values and long-term goals rather than being driven solely by immediate impulses or external pressures.

Blowing in the wind—reacting to life—often feels like surrendering control. We let circumstances dictate our mood, direction, and sense of self. This reactive state can be easy to slip into, but it can also lead to feelings of helplessness, anxiety, or dissatisfaction as we're constantly chasing external stability in an inherently dynamic world.

We can break this cycle by anchoring in the present and teaching ourselves to respond, not react. When faced with challenges, we can take a moment to step back, observe our emotions, and make choices rooted in clarity rather than confusion. It empowers us to act purposefully, even in the face of uncertainty.

In *Walden,* Henry David Thoreau explained, "I went to the woods because I wished to live deliberately, to front only the essential facts of life, and see if I could not learn what it had to teach, and not, when I came to die, discover that I had not lived."

Thoreau urges readers to live with purpose and mindfulness, focusing on what truly matters rather than being consumed by distractions. By adopting this mindset, we shift from passive participants to active creators of our path. We move with intention, grounded in self-awareness, and are better equipped to navigate life's inevitable ups and downs. Instead of being blown aimlessly from one issue to another, we become the steady tree, bending with life's currents but rooted deeply in our inner strength and purpose.

Physical health is deeply connected to mental and emotional well-being. Regular exercise, a balanced diet, quality sleep, and relaxation techniques like yoga or meditation can all support inner peace. Inner peace often eludes those who rely on others' opinions for self-worth. Cultivate self-acceptance and recognize that your value isn't dependent on external success or approval. For some, prayer, meditation, or journaling provides a sense of connection to something greater than themselves. Reflecting on your purpose and values can bring clarity and peace.

Be kind to yourself and create an environment of self-compassion. Spending time in nature can help you feel grounded and calm. Walking in the park, hiking, or simply sitting under a tree, connecting with the natural world, brings peace and perspective.

Treat yourself with the same patience and understanding you would offer a dear friend (or a student!). Finding inner peace involves self-awareness, acceptance, and a sense of harmony within yourself. Being fully present in the moment can reduce stress and quiet the mental chatter. Focusing on your breath, sensations, or surroundings without judgment can help you accept life as it is rather than resisting or fearing it.

Inner peace comes from letting go of the need to control everything. Accepting uncertainty and impermanence allows you to focus on what truly matters and respond calmly to challenges. Recognizing and appreciating the positive aspects of life shifts your perspective and helps you focus on abundance rather than lack. Some of the happiest people own very little of material value, yet they enjoy their lives immensely, celebrating family, loved ones and milestones along the way.

Holding onto resentment or anger disrupts inner peace. Disconnection between your actions and your core values creates inner conflict. Inner peace is not about the absence of conflict or challenges, but about developing flexibility and perspective to navigate them gracefully. Forgiving others—and yourself—frees you from the emotional weight of past hurts.

Focusing on one's blessings tends to increase contentment and happiness. Gratitude encourages people to appreciate life's small delights, from the beauty of nature to the companionship of loved ones. There is joy to be found in simplicity and connecting with others.

No matter what life brings, never compromise your core values. In his essay, *Self-Reliance,* American author and poet Ralph Waldo Emerson wrote:

> "Insist on yourself. *Never imitate.* Your own gift you can present every moment with the cumulative force of a while life's cultivation; but *of the adopted talent of another,* you have only an extemporaneous, half possession."

Ultimately, a life lived well leaves a legacy of love, resilience, and positive impact, offering both personal fulfillment and a contribution to the world around us. Emerson wisely knew that the most meaningful way to achieve fulfillment is to live a life true to oneself rather than conform to societal pressures.

In my view, living well is not a single achievement but a collection of experiences and attitudes that give life meaning and joy. We can live well not by seeking perfection but by embracing purpose, growth, compassion, connection, and gratitude. Whether through small acts of kindness, lifelong learning, or meaningful connections (use those calling cards!), we can create a life that feels worthwhile to us and valuable to others.

Who inspires you as an example of living well? Why not inspire yourself? You have one wonderful life to live, and I hope that my story inspires you to take advantage of all of the precious gifts that life has to offer. I have experienced the many joys of family, friendship, community, travel, and art; and these joys await you as well.

Go out and *grab* life, soak up *every* fantastical sunbeam, and reflect it into the world. Live in alignment with your values, build meaningful connections, and leave this beautiful, diverse, ever-changing world better than you found it.

PUBLISHER'S NOTE

Flourishing Media is the non-profit imprint of Partners Media. As a purpose-driven publishing program, Flourishing Media amplifies the importance of the arts and entrepreneurship to our community in Winston-Salem and beyond.

Local talent will create, design, produce, sell, distribute, and warehouse our titles. The Arts Council of Winston-Salem and Forsyth County acts as our fiscal sponsor, making donations tax-deductible. All revenue from these books will be donated to recipients chosen by the author. Donations have covered costs for production, marketing, printing, and distribution. As directed by the author, the revenue will benefit the University of North Carolina School of the Arts, Salem College, and the Howell Binkley Fellowship Program.

A Life Well Lived has received generous support from Dr. and Mrs. Malcolm Brown, Lynn and Barry Eisenberg, the Mastroianni-Shaw Fund, Janie and J.D. Wilson, and the Arts Council of Winston-Salem and Forsyth County.

It is published in association with:
Fifth Letter - *www.fifth-letter.com*
Excalibur Direct Marketing - *www.excaliburdirect.com*
Thomas L. Spry

We are honored and grateful for the participation of:
Ben Folds, *Genre-defying Musician, Composer, and Storyteller*
David Parsons, *Founder, Artistic Director & Choreographer, Parsons Dance*
Susan Jaffe, *Artistic Director, American Ballet Theatre*
Michael Wilson, *Broadway Director*

ABOUT THE AUTHORS

Phyllis Dunning has been a beloved English literature teacher to thousands of students in Winston-Salem, North Carolina, over the course of her 33-year career in education. Throughout her inspiring life, she has traveled the globe, nurtured lasting relationships with students, artists, and friends, and championed the arts at every level. Phyllis has generously supported numerous cultural institutions, including the Winston-Salem Symphony, Piedmont Opera, the University of North Carolina School of the Arts, and Reynolda House Museum of American Art.

Joyce Storey is an award-winning, New York City—based writer, actor, and producer, and a close friend of Phyllis Dunning for many years. Besides collaborating with Phyllis, she has written plays—including *Caged* and *Time Wars*—and is the co-author of two books, *75 Monologues Kids Will Love!* and *101 Awesome Original Monologues for 20-Somethings*. Joyce is the President of Bentley Productions, a theatrical lighting company representing the designs of Tony Award-winning Howell Binkley, and she sits on the board of Parsons Dance. She enjoys traveling, entertaining, and writing.